About the author

John Gloster-Smith, BA, PGCE, MAHPP, AC-accred., lives in Wiltshire, UK with his wife Akasha Lonsdale, who is a psychotherapist and Interfaith Minister. He has two grown-up sons. He is essentially an educator and this manifests as a life and executive coach, a group facilitator, a trainer and a teacher. He studied Modern History at Oxford and was a teacher for 17 years. He then left to embark on an extensive programme in his own self-development in Humanistic and Transpersonal psychology and Eastern philosophy. He found particular inspiration in Gestalt Therapy while training at Metanoia Psychotherapy Training Institute in London and then in Siddha Yoga with Gurumayi Chidvilasananda, although his approach is much more eclectic and holistic than those two influences. He built a business with his wife called The Empowering Partnership, subsequently extending its activities to include Laughter Yoga under "The Laughter School" logo, and he leads personal and spiritual development programmes, gives coaching, writes and gives talks to a wide range of audiences.

Connecting to Inner Peace

Your direct line to contentment

By

John Gloster-Smith

EP BOOKS
Wiltshire

First published in Great Britain in 2010 by EP Books

© John Gloster-Smith 2010

The right of John Gloster-Smith to be identified as the author has been asserted by him in accordance with Section 77 and 78 of the Copyright, Designs and Patents Act 1988. He asserts and gives notice of his moral right under this Act.

All rights reserved. No part of this book may be reproduced, stored in a retrieval system or transmitted in any form by any means (electronic or mechanical, through reprography, digital transmission, recording or otherwise) without the prior permission of the publisher at the address below, except as in accordance with the provisions of the Copyright, Designs and Patents Act 1988.

The intent of the author is to offer information of a general nature to help you in your quest for emotional and spiritual well-being. In the event that you use any of the information in this book for yourself, which is your right, the author and publisher assume no responsibility for your actions. Any advice or suggestions must be checked out with any relevant qualified professional before action is taken. This particularly, but not exclusively, applies to any legal, financial or medical decisions you make.

EP Books, 21 Fynamore Gardens, Calne, Wiltshire SN11 0UA, UK
Tel: +44(0)1249 813 188; john@johnglostersmith.com
www.johnglostersmith.com

ISBN-13: 978-0-9546908-1-6

British Library cataloguing-in-publication Data

A CIP record for this book is available from the British Library

Cover designed by Beatrice Buchser, Uniik Visual Communication, Zurich, Switzerland. www.uniik.com
Photograph by Neil Clarke

Printed and bound in Great Britain by
CPI Antony Rowe, Chippenham and Eastbourne
www.antonyrowe.co.uk

Dedication

This book is dedicated to my wife Akasha,
who is a true inspiration in my life.

Contents

Foreword	11
Introduction	13
PART 1: BECOMING AWARE	**19**
Introducing Awareness	20
Awareness	23
Being aware	23
Noticing what's going on	25
How deeply are you aware?	27
With your mind	28
Sensing and feeling: making contact	30
Contemplation	32
Meditation	35
As a tool for self-awareness	37
Knowing more of yourself	37
The present moment	39
The point of awareness is a "now" event	39
Pause and become present	40
Witnessing your mental stream	41
Is it useful?	43
Tips for anchoring your awareness in the "Now"	43
Taking responsibility	46
Responsibility is response-ability	46
Honesty	48
Choosing your reality	50
We create our own reality	50
The beliefs we choose and the part they play	50
We can change our experience	51
The difference between believing and knowing	53

Contents

Being aware — 54

PART 2: IS THIS WHO YOU REALLY ARE? — 55

Managing your mind — 56

What you think, you are — 58
- What is "the mind"? — 58
- What we believe manifests in our lives — 59
- We can choose our own preferred reality — 61

You are not your Past — 62
- How we learned all this stuff — 62
- Parent and child styles in adulthood — 62
- It influences our perceptions of the world and ourselves — 63
- You are not your past — 64
- We can change what we have grown up with — 65
- We chose this life to learn what we needed to learn — 65

Perception — 68
- Interpretations: what we've made the world mean — 68
- Perception and knowledge — 69

Feelings — 71
- Anger — 71
- Sadness — 72
- Fear — 72
- More complex feelings — 73
- Love — 74
- Love versus fear — 75
- Letting go of disruptive feelings — 75

Thoughts and feelings — 77
- Patterns of thoughts — 77
- Compulsive — 78

The guilt cycle — 80
- Right/wrong — 80
- Judgements — 81

Contents

Blame	81
Guilt	81
Failure	82
Punishment	82
Shame	82
Resentment	**84**
Holding on to past wrongs	84
How it eats away: bitterness	85
Letting go	85
Anxiety and worry	**88**
The worry habit	88
What it does to your body	88
Manifesting what you fear	89
Using present-moment awareness	89
Desire and need	**91**
Expectations	91
Jealousy	92
"There's not enough"	93
Focus on the feeling	94
Beliefs	**96**
Beliefs about yourself	97
Self-esteem: loving and valuing yourself	99
Self-esteem actions	99
Valuing/loving others	103
Separation	**104**
Letting go again	**106**
PART 3: KNOWING YOUR INNER SELF	**109**
What dwells within us	**110**
The Ego and the Real Self	**111**
The Ego as the limited self	111
The "small" self and the "great" Self	111

Contents

The Self	**114**
More on the small self and great Self	114
Some characteristics of the Great Self	115
Maps of consciousness	**118**
Ken Wilber	118
Spiral dynamics	120
Some other thinkers	122
Ego characteristics	**123**
Qualities of the ego	123
An interplay within yourself	129
Developing skill	**130**
From Ego to the Great Self	**131**
Developing your sense of "I"	131
The universal I am	133
The inner journey	135
Living as I am	135
Developing your centre of awareness	**136**
Managing your mind: the constant practice	137
The gap	138
Physical awareness	139
Witnessing	142
Detachment and surrender	142
Re-connection	144
Being with other people	144
Being present	145
I am That	146
PART 4: IN THE REAL WORLD	**149**
The Real World	**150**
How do you show up?	151
Will	**154**
Trust	**157**

How much do you trust?	157
It is a choice	158
From trusting to knowing	159

Having vision and purpose — 161

Visioning the life you want	162
Living intentionally	164
Coming from deep purpose	170

With other people — 171

Relationship as the highest practice	171
The Shadow	171
Making others responsible	175
Love and needing love	176
Fear-based relating	178
Patterns of relating: Seeing the rackets	178
Healing wounds	180
Changing your ways of relating	180
Looking for the jewel	181

Work, money and career — 183

Work and vocation	183
Money as an ego trap	184
Being aware with money	186
Being on purpose in your work	187

Practice — 190

Self-discipline	190
Life laundry	193

The journey — 195

What will you choose?	195
Facing and accepting its challenges	196
Confronting your demons	196
Re-member and re-mind yourself	197

Further reading — 199

Further information	201

Foreword

This book was originally written for people attending my programmes and therefore for those who were clearly interested in developing themselves and had probably already started down that path. My intention was to provide some further information and explanation about what I was teaching and some practical tools and techniques, as well as further insights to support them on their path. It has since become clear to me that there are actually very many who have already been dabbling in self-help or self-improvement and are looking for some greater insight or awareness that will help them really move forward or go deeper.

At the same time it seems that people want learnings that are practical and grounded. Thus this book is written as a practical aid, to help people learn more about themselves and about how to achieve a breakthrough to a higher level of living. After all, it is not just about studying ideas but also about how you live every day that real, tangible change is achieved. There are too many people out there dabbling with ideas, quickly moving on to the next allegedly "new" thing, but not actually addressing the real issues that are getting in the way of a truly fulfilling life.

This book is all about supporting you to become aware and take responsibility for your personal growth. It is all about making personal choices. The approach adopted sits firmly within the western humanistic and transpersonal tradition. It also draws upon eastern philosophy, particularly that in Indian yoga, and seeks to integrate eastern and western thinking. The intention is that the concepts will empower you.

Included in this material is a focus on spirituality, since the view is taken that as humans we are also spiritual beings with spiritual needs. Current western civilisation has been focused on a materialistic path for too long now and it is not serving us. However, what you do with that is up to you. This is about awakening to who we are. Thus in writing about spiritual matters, there is no particular religious dogma or axe to grind. Rather I would hope to support personal

Foreword

empowerment and choice, in whatever way that is meaningful for you personally.

This book is not the product just of me. It comes out of the flow of Awareness of which I am a part, and therefore of what is unmanifest as well as what is manifest. It comes from a lifetime of teaching and personal learning and growth. It therefore comes from all the people who taught me, those whom I lived and worked with, all the very many people I have taught, trained, coached and mentored, my professional colleagues, my friends, my fellow trainees, participants with me on workshops and courses, and the wonderful myriad of humanity that it has been my privilege to encounter. All have been my teachers.

I would particularly like to acknowledge and thank the following people for their help and support over time as this book has gone through various gestations. First and foremost I want to thank my wife Akasha Lonsdale for her wonderful support and inspiration, the time spent in listening and in offering suggestions, and the reading of the text. I also want to acknowledge my friend Gordon Glass for his time in providing support and in the many hours we have spent discussing many of the concepts in this book.

Introduction

Many people are seeking a way forward, to gain a real meaning to their lives, a purpose that has a fundamental ring of truth to it, one that expresses who they are, rather than the superficialities of current material existence. This is no mere trend of the moment. It is affecting whole swathes of our society and it is global. Something profound is going on.

At the time of publication, our civilisation appears to be at a crucial turning point. We have just encountered a massive global financial crisis and our economic life went almost to the brink of collapse. This in itself has been a shock to many. However, we also have a growing crisis at a planetary level, such as widespread extinctions of animal species, loss of forests, shrinkage of ice caps, sea level rise, pressure on resources, desertification, water shortage, population growth and hunger. We may be threatened by climate change on a huge scale. This too is seen as threatening, but this time to our very existence on this planet. It is like we are outgrowing our planet but have not fully grown up ourselves and become holistically responsible.

No wonder people ask, "What is the point?" At the same time, people are discovering that our much-prized material existence that we cling to actually doesn't on its own "work". It cannot "work", if we live life at a faster and faster pace, suffer more depression, feel stressed, experience family breakdown, live in crowded cities, chase work that doesn't satisfy and experience loneliness and unhappiness in the midst of apparent plenty.

What we have in my view is poverty of spirit.

Not surprisingly therefore, people are looking for something new, something that finally "does it" for them. But what exactly that is, isn't clear to them.

Introduction

Eckhart Tolle[1] says that what we have now is a crisis of Ego. According to him the Ego is the illusory self, who we think we are, and the source of our suffering as humans. We have reached a point where we are poised to break through to another level of existence. What we need to do is to "awaken" and see and know who we really are. When people reach such transition points *en masse*, it can feel like things are getting worse. The contradictions in existence are being heightened, but now so that we can become aware and choose.

This book is written to facilitate that process of awakening, to help others to know and be who we really are.

My own view is that a part of us, our higher selves, what I call our Self with a capital "S" to make the difference clear, already knows who we really are. However the unaware part of us, which I call our "small" self or Ego self, that part of us which is still living in the mundane material world, has not caught up with that yet. What we need to do is to learn to **connect** the two, to create a bridge between our Ego self and our "great" Self.

Only then will the apparent contradictions revealed in the crisis facing humanity and the planet, of which we are supposed to be the guardians, be resolved. The split in our consciousness will then be healed and we will discover who we really are, that we are really in fact all One. The beauty of this is that we won't be told this; we won't have it imposed on us. We will simply know it from within, each in our own way, authentically, and the divisions within us and between us and between the different components of the planet with disappear.

So this book is all about that connecting, learning to become aware, to make contact with our inner Selves, to discover that truth, that inner peace, contentment and ultimately that love that is really us. It is also about learning to distinguish, to be aware of our Ego self, to know when we are acting from our Ego self and to distinguish between our Ego self and the real or "great" Self. Since the Ego is so deeply ingrained, we need techniques and practice to help us to unlearn old habits and acquire other more fulfilling ones.

---

[1] Eckhart Tolle, *The New Earth*, New York, Penguin, 2005, p. 258.

Introduction

Thus in **Part 1**, we start with the basic building blocks in the discovery of who we are, through using the power of **Awareness**. We explore how to awaken, how to become aware through a series of awareness techniques and approaches. These are core skills that you can use as you work through the rest of the book. Then in **Part 2** we ask the question "Is this who you really are?" and conduct an enquiry into who we think we are. We look at how the mind works, the Ego self at work. We will look at those places where we tend to take ourselves, especially those places we don't really want to go to, and how we create the experience that life is somehow not working for us. This also includes suggestions for managing your mind and letting go of some of those aspects that no longer serve you. Then, in **Part 3** you are introduced to the nature of the Self, that deeper Self that lies somewhere inside you and that, although masked by the Ego self, is who you are. You will be able to identify some classic Ego behaviours, explore in more depth the nature of the "great" Self and learn how you might build your awareness and connection with your real Self. Finally in **Part 4**, we look at how you live the life you have, in the so-called real world, and at some techniques and approaches that will make for realising what is being discussed in this book in everyday situations.

It is through transcending this so-called "reality" that you will embrace the new. It is here and now that the shift can occur, in what you are doing, in what occurs in your life and are aware of moment by moment. What is needed is to become aware of what the present really contains. That sounds like a paradox, and it is. The present contains all the gems, all the riches, all the possibility that life really offers us. It is not "out there" that life has its gift for us. It is not in the pursuit of something new, some possession, some idea, some person, some place, or some guru. It is right here, inside, in the beauty of who you are. So, come and take a long, slow, gentle, loving look.

Introduction

Using this book

First of all, I don't advise rushing through this book and then putting it on your shelves with the others with the thought, "OK, I've done that one too". Moving on from one thing to the next, looking for something new, is an ego pattern that is prevalent at present, where we don't pause, don't stop and ask, **"What is going on right now?"** In this book, you will be encouraged to pause and ask that question, again and again. This book is intended to be worked through gradually, with reflection and use of the exercises, or "activities". A lot of the material is actually deceptively subtle, and it pays to re-read and reflect on various parts of it. You might find yourself going back to earlier bits with new ideas. So, take your time.

The book has been divided into chapters and each chapter is divided into sections for easy reading. The structure has been deliberately chosen. The logical flow of the book starts in the first part with awareness and how you can develop it. The implications and applications of that are then explored in the rest of the book. Thus I think you will find that it pays to work through the book from beginning to end to get the full impact, rather than dipping in here and there.

There are a lot of what I have called "activities" at various points, which I have put in to enable you to reflect on what you have read and apply the material to yourself. In the process you will in effect be developing your own awareness and skill.

I would suggest that you also have your own note-taking system to jot things down as you go through the book. A lot of people who do their own self-development use a **journal** to help them. Thus they write about their awarenesses and insights day by day and reflect on what they are discovering. This can be very powerful.

Some take journaling a step further and use it to write down all that they are aware of on a given aspect of themselves, to really go into it and in the process discover something about themselves that will help them move forward. That might also be helpful for you.

Introduction

You will note that there is a fair degree of repetition of the basic methodology of developing and using awareness in the early and middle parts of the book. This is no mere accident, since when we work with self-awareness it often pays to revisit the techniques we are using. The ego has a subtle knack of pulling us back to the "known and familiar" rather than the growth path you have chosen. Hence revisiting the principles is designed to reinforce the learning process.

Part 1: Becoming aware

Introducing Awareness

I am going to invite you to be aware of what is going on, consciously aware of what is happening moment by moment. I am suggesting that you notice your own process, what occurs in you moment by moment. It is perfectly simple and utterly profound. It is your key to heaven, and one you have always had.

Humans have this capability but have become very capable of ignoring it. Such is the effect of the vicissitudes of life.

Awareness is central to anything you might do in making changes or developing yourself. Put simply, if you don't understand what you are doing, thinking, feeling, or sensing, how can you change it? Awareness work has been called "the therapy of the obvious". Except that it isn't obvious to you at the time! You're missing "it" and you need to "get it", to become aware.

Thus we speak of people who live unconsciously, unaware of some aspect of what they are doing. Their awareness is limited to the surface of their lives, governed by habits acquired over a lifetime. They learned to live that way from when they were very small, adapting at each point to what they needed to do to get by, to survive. It seemed the way things were done, and it probably worked. They might have liked things to be a bit different but didn't see any need to do anything about it.

Or at least it worked until they hit a point where the status quo was no longer acceptable. This might have been a crisis in their lives or it could have been a slow process that led them to a point where they decided that things needed to change.

This could be such things as an illness, an accident, a job loss, a bereavement, divorce or separation in a relationship, financial problems, robbery, reaching a certain age in life, the menopause, or any of what people might consider as life-changing events. It could be a gradual realisation. For example, I broke up with my first wife, entered a period of warring with her over the children, lost my mother

Introducing awareness

and had people around me succumbing to cancer over a 3 year period. My life felt dead, numb, and meaningless. I eventually decided that at least some of this was down to me and I needed to make changes.

The point of realisation is one way this comes to us. For some it is like an awakening, as though someone has just come and shone a light on a whole lot of murky stuff in the over-crowded attic or loft of our lives, and found that it needs clearing out.

Then as you start to probe, you find all sorts of things going on, things you hadn't realised about yourself and other people. Crucially in terms of personal development as I see it, this includes what you've been doing and what part you've been playing in what's been happening. What you find might seem negative, but if you do it "right" you'll also find all sorts of positive, uplifting things too.

I say "right" not in the sense of obedience to some rulebook but in the sense of making choices that serve you, as opposed to ones that don't. So, I'm not talking about doing years of therapy that probes into your past, unless of course you want to do that. There's nothing "wrong" with you or me. At our essence, we're perfect. We just don't see it. I'm talking about developing awareness so as to be able to notice what you are doing that does not serve you and then to let it go. The sort of awareness that is discussed in these pages is one where you can also be aware of that deeper, more connected, more profound, more spiritually and personally at-one part of you. This is a part that is truly who you are, one that feels good, wholesome, alive, contented, powerful, enthusiastic, warm, playful, and whatever else it takes - a part that in a way only you will know feels "right".

This is a very positive stance on life and on our potential as humans. It stands in stark contrast to many beliefs current in our civilisation, but it is central to where we are headed. For example, it is perfectly possible to centre your awareness, to so manage your mind that you can focus one-pointedly on what uplifts you and enables you to feel joy and contentment. Our minds have the potential for us to experience pure heaven right now. We don't have to die to get that. It is already here right now. We have that gift already. We can just become aware of it.

Thus we will start by exploring a range of tools to develop **self-awareness** as a key first step to managing the mind. The aim is to work towards a steady state of equilibrium or centredness where you are not caught up in what occurs and are not thrown off course. Additionally you can use these methods to recover your equilibrium after some upset or irritation. In that steady state, you can move to experiencing more joy and effectiveness in your life.

These tools are very simple, simple even to the point of obviousness, and yet so simple that we've become very skilled at ignoring them. However in their implications they are very profound. Bear in mind that in reality you are simply remembering old skills, since at our core we are already complete. We just need to see through the veil of our ego to the truth of that, each in our own way, according to our own path in life.

Awareness

To be truly aware is to be truly alive. We are not talking about the mere fact of thinking or existing. We are talking here about the quality of our experience: our capacity to be fully in the moment, to admire the beauty of our surroundings, to breathe the sweetness of the air, to hear the sounds of the birds and the wind in the trees, to sense the sheer joy of this moment, to enjoy the presence of a friend, to spontaneously laugh and to feel the pleasure in your body and the opening of your heart, to love the very moment that you are here now with all your being. Very many of us do not have this aliveness.

To cultivate awareness is central to managing your mind and to personal growth. In fact it is absolutely crucial. Not only is it a sure route to enhancing your quality of life by getting you more in touch with yourself, but as I said before you also need to be aware of what you do if you are to change it. Self-awareness enables you to **catch** your patterns of thinking, feeling and behaviour that are getting in your way.

So, to help you enhance your awareness, we will now study a series of awareness techniques.

Being aware

At the level of the mundane, this might seem obvious. Surely as humans, we "think". Stuff goes on in our heads. Our minds are active, for many of us too active for our comfort. Therefore we are aware. However, one might point out that we are so pre-occupied with the detail of our lives that we don't actually notice a lot of this mental activity. It just goes on and on. We're on a form of mental autopilot.

You might also think, surely we are aware of our surroundings and of ourselves. Except that often we aren't. For example there is your body which might contain certain sensations, ones that you might be aware of if you attended to them. These sensations might contain messages for you. For example you might feel a certain feeling in your body as you focus on carrying out a physical task and if you attended to the

Becoming aware

energy you might become aware that there is a danger that you had not previously noticed. Something was telling you.

How much are you aware of all your senses: touch, smell, hearing, taste, and seeing? And are you really aware of your feelings? You might for example feel a level of anxiety as you undertake a task as to whether you can complete it in time. A lot of people habitually disconnect from their feelings. You might be able to "do" emotion pretty well, and even say how you feel about something. However, this can be superficial. In awareness work, it is often about learning to be aware of the subtle feelings and sensations that flow through us, clues to a deeper reality.

As humans we are also potentially aware at more subtle levels. For example, I might be aware of my intuition, knowing something but without having worked it out. Something just came into my mind, a gut feeling perhaps. I might just know that something is so, even if I might not have any tangible evidence of it. Also, I might sense what others might be feeling, even if I can't see them or hear them. I might know the truth of someone's experience, even though they've said nothing. As my awareness expands, I might feel a connection with others in a room, or with what is behind me and outside my actual field of vision, or with nature or even with the world at large. I might even know what is happening for another even if I'm not with them. People in close relationships for example often report how they have both simultaneously thought something even when apart. In case you are sceptical, then observe what animals do, such as a pet dog does in anticipating our return home[2]. When I was a child, our pet spaniel at home would work up a frenzy as my father walked the 10 minutes from the station.

Such awareness is vital. This is our route to having our heart sing. Being fully connected to awareness puts us firmly in touch with the most profound gifts that life has to offer, gifts we already have innately. With this awareness I might for example for no particular reason and with no effort just start to feel a sensation in my heart area

---

[2] Rupert Sheldrake, *Dogs that know when their owners are coming home and other unexplained powers of animals*, London, Arrow Books, 2000.

that feels uplifting. A warm glow may start to flow through my body, not necessarily directed at a particular person, just simply a pure loving feeling. It is just there, happening within us, a pure gift of being human. No wonder people report that at times they feel "in love with life".

We are conscious in more ways than we acknowledge. When we contact our higher levels of consciousness, we start to tap into an awareness that has far greater power than the mundane. Awareness is utterly accessible, perfectly simple, right there, so to speak, in front of us. It simply involves an allowing, a shift in perception to tap more into it. How do we do this?

Noticing what's going on

To tap into our awareness, all we have to do is to stop our preoccupations - and **pause**. Yes, stop and pause. So many of us are hectically engaged with the everyday detail of our lives, wrapped up in it all, that we're cutting ourselves off from big chunks of our awareness. So we need to pause.

Activity: Awareness

So, stop....pause....become aware of your breathing. Take in a breath, a deep breath, let it out slowly and relax some of your body as you do so. Do this again. Allow yourself to take several further breaths, relaxing more and more. Then allow your awareness to focus on an object. Contemplate it for a few moments, just taking it in. Then become aware of any thoughts that are in your mind. Just notice them. There's no need to judge or assess or interpret them. Just notice them. Then notice anything that is going on around you, in the same way, like hearing sounds. And then bring your awareness back to your breathing. Take one or two deeper breaths and then come back to reading this.

All you were doing is relaxing so that you could heighten your awareness of what was going on in your field of awareness. Then you

Becoming aware

were simply focusing your awareness on a particular object, on your thoughts and on your surroundings.

What was that like? Was it an effort? Did you get distracted in any way whilst doing that activity? Did your mind start thinking about something? Most of us are so wrapped up in our minds, in an incessant stream of thinking, in a kind of mental busyness, that we don't notice what's actually happening inside us, like just breathing, or what we are feeling, or what is around us. We don't pause and just tune in to it.

Activity: Awareness 2

So, for practice, spend a few moments regularly to get the benefit. Start, as we did, by breathing a few deeper breaths so as to focus and relax, and then spend a little while noticing what's happening inside you....and then.... what's happening around you. If you find you get wrapped up in some chain of thought about it, just notice those thoughts and then bring your awareness back to just noticing.

Write down your experiences:
....
....
....
....
....
....
....
....
....
....

It takes practice to unlearn old habits. Notice how often your awareness gets distracted. This is something we will attend to later on. The idea for the moment is just to practice noticing what is going on in your field of awareness.

Awareness

How deeply are you aware?

Most people have relatively superficial levels of awareness. Partly this might be because it has not occurred to them to take a look. However, this may also be because their awareness is blunted to some extent by their life experiences.

Three common forms of limited awareness are:

1. Deflection

Here we shift our attention away to something else. A common form of this is changing the subject in conversation away from something awkward, where we might feel uncomfortable. However, the point is that we are not aware that we are doing it. We don't want to go there. So we go somewhere else. We deflect the energy away from a painful area on to something less challenging. In time this becomes ingrained and habitual.

2. De-sensitisation

This is not sensing or feeling something. Here, awareness is probably blunted. A person might simply not be aware of how he feels. When asked what he feels he replies with what is in effect a thought instead: "I think I feel..." He might be unable to describe his feelings simply because they are outside his awareness.

3. Projection

In this case, we direct the energy on to somebody or something else, when in truth it belongs to us, at least in part. So, we think somebody else displays the behaviour or the characteristics, when in fact they are also ours too. For example, you might think that your boss is very critical, when actually you have a critical side to you too that you don't acknowledge. Often others say in response to a projection on to another, "Oh, but you can be like that too!"

Becoming aware

To expand awareness, we need to practice the skills of attending to our experiences, as was described above. The key is to be able to get a handle on what it is that is outside your awareness. This is about sharpening your acuity. We will address this in more detail in later stages of the book. For the moment, simply start to ask yourself what it is that you do not fully attend to. Use the technique of pausing, breathing and going within that was described in the last section.

- For **deflection** it is about beginning to notice what it is that is uncomfortable that you want to turn away from. It might just lie at the edge of your awareness. You might already know but aren't admitting it!

- For **desensitisation**, it is about developing your sensing, and it can be helpful to start by taking time out to relax your body and to tune into what your body is feeling (see "Sensing and Feeling" below). Ask yourself, "How do I feel about this?" or "What might I feel about this?"

- For **projection**, this is more complex but in brief involves asking yourself: when you notice a quality or behaviour in someone else, what are you being reminded of that is a part of you? It might be a quality that you do not want to own. You might notice that you feel something about it, which is a further clue, such as a reaction that you are not comfortable with. We explore this further in the chapter in Part 4 entitled "With other people".

With your mind

What we are doing with these techniques to sharpen awareness is in effect using our minds to serve us instead of work against our own best interests. It is an exercise in will and choice, choosing to direct our awareness in particular directions. We will explore more of this too later.

One way of developing awareness is learning to **focus** your mind inwardly to contemplate or attend to whatever is going on. What we are doing here is using awareness to listen to the wisdom of the body and to use what is inside us to tell us what is there for us to learn.

Activity: Focusing on your body awareness

Take in a few deeper breaths and allow yourself to relax. Now as you do this, allow your awareness to follow your breath. As you breathe in, notice your awareness is drawn inwards as it follows the breath in to the chest. As you breathe out let your muscles relax. With each in-breath, allow your attention to rest inwards. Keep that attention in your chest or further down in your stomach. Now see what's there when you ask, "What is really going on for me right now?" Sense inside. Sense what's there. Don't get into thinking about it. Just notice whatever is there.

Select one thing that comes up to focus on. Stay with it and work to see if you can get a *felt sense* of it. You might need to practice going within like this to get used to it and to what is going on inside. However, for this exercise, just allow yourself to notice a particular sensation and stay with it.

Ask yourself what is the *quality* of that felt sense. Let a word, phrase or image come up. Let this be spontaneous; don't question or analyse it. You are working with your inner wisdom, and reason and analysis don't necessarily help at this point. Stay with it till you have a word, phrase or image that fits.

Go back and forth between the felt sense and the quality and check how they resonate with each other. If the quality fits, then you might get a body sense, or it just seems right like a sort of conviction, like you just "know" it. If it doesn't fit, you can change either the felt sense or the quality till it does fit.

For example, you might be simply feeling very uncomfortable about something and are just aware that you are churned up. Yet when you go inside and explore the feeling, you might get words like "gutted" or "butterflies" and as a result you would be able to see whether you are feeling very sad about something or actually very anxious. If you then asked yourself what that real feeling is about, you might then get a lot clearer about what has sparked your internal reaction, what the real issue is.

This process can be repeated to further clarify the issue; you might on occasions need to give yourself a fair amount of time. At others, with skill, it might become a quick self-check, going within to ask what's there for you to get and trusting the answer that comes.

This process is based loosely on "Focusing", a method developed by Eugene Gendlin, and it is a particularly effective technique to use in the early stages of developing awareness[3].

Sensing and feeling: making contact

As you go further within yourself, you will start to develop finer skills in sensing and feeling. It is very possible that feelings will come up that you may need to deal with. We cover this more in later parts of this book. It could be you will find that developing awareness is the tool you need to recognise any unfinished business from the past or in dealing with current situations. Once you are aware of these feelings, you can work to release them. As suggested in Part 2 in relation to emotions, if they reoccur you will also need to develop skill in becoming less attached to these feelings and in letting them go.

What you will also be doing is making contact with what are probably highly under-developed abilities within you. Not only will you be able to contact finer awarenesses within you but you will probably find you can sense and feel more in relation to what's going on in the world around you. You may, for example, start to sense how others might be feeling and be more able to empathise with them. Daniel Goleman[4] argues that the key competency that people often need to develop at work is Social Awareness, the ability to sense where others are coming from, our "social radar". It is very noticeable how people who really get into self-improvement develop a very fine ability to sense

---

[3] Gendlin, *Focusing*, New York/Toronto, Bantam Books, 1981
[4] Daniel Goleman, *Working with Emotional Intelligence*, London edition, Bloomsbury, 1998

others' emotional states. Not that most of us actually "know". We need to check it out and we may not be accurate. However, you may just have a hunch that hits the nail on the head.

When you are more finely aware, you may find you can make closer contact with others and draw others to you. However this may also depend on the level of authenticity, of truth, in you. We will explore that later too. Getting more closely in contact with how you feel, and being ready to own and express that, plays a big part. You will need good awareness to do that.

A relaxation activity

Here is another practice that can help you become more aware. It involves relaxation, which as we've seen is very necessary given the very stressed lives many of us are living, but it then enables us to sense through using our bodies. Very often, I find that before I can work really effectively with someone I first need to invite them to relax. Then they can more easily connect.

Activity: Relaxation

Find somewhere to lie down, where you won't be disturbed. Take a few deeper breaths as before, but now use the in-breath to breathe, in your mind's eye, into any tense areas in your body and then as you breathe out have a sense that you are in some way relaxing those muscles....

Now, take your attention to your feet, to your toes..... Tell your toes to relax....Maybe breathe, so to speak, into the toes....Or tighten your toes up or deliberately tense them and then relax them as much as you can.....Or stretch them out

Now go on to your feet, to the muscles in the feet and do the same, then your ankles....And gradually work your way up your body.....Really take time over this....Don't hurry - that's what we are all doing, hurrying. Just focus on the area and relax it.

When you reach your torso, work up the front and then up the back, carefully. Remember to tighten and release your buttocks and your stomach muscles in particular.

Then go to your fingers and up your arms

Now, you can attend to your shoulders and your neck

And now go to your face. Pay particular attention to your mouth area and your smiling muscles. In the English-speaking culture we do a lot of smiling – and hold a lot of tension there. Also have you heard of the expression "tight-lipped", because we hold on to our feelings?

When you've finished, just lie there and enjoy the relaxation for a few moments. You could even meditate there, if you wish.

Then, take one or two deeper breaths and bring your awareness very gently back into the room and, when you are ready, sit up.

What people find when they first do this activity is that they discover areas in their body that they did not know were tense – and can hold pain. It may be physical pain and also emotional pain. This pain may be connected to feelings, thoughts and behaviours that need to be released. The psychologist Wilhelm Reich said that muscles have memories. At least you are now aware of what is there. That is the first step to healing.

There are other ways of tackling deeper feelings locked in the body. There are many body therapies available. One such approach is called Rolfing, another is Hellerwork and a third is the Alexander Technique. The first two of these involve deep tissue massage. Do get advice before you proceed further, though, and check with a doctor if you have a medical condition.

Contemplation

People often call this connecting process, "being in tune" with yourself. To do this, we need to give ourselves space and time to slow

Awareness

down and be still. Another way to do this is by contemplation. This practice is used very widely in various spiritual traditions to get in touch with and explore what's happening inside.

With contemplation, what we are doing is sustaining steady, wordless attention on a particular topic, puzzle, or object. We are not thinking about it. What is happening is that we are tapping into more subtle levels of awareness, which are sensed, intuited, even "known" in a way that we cannot rationally explain. We are by-passing the thinking mind's chatter, not trying to use the analytical side that tries to work it out.

The key stages in contemplation are:

1. **Selecting the topic or object**: It may be anything; perhaps an object, a special person, a question, a problem, or some phrase that you want to hold in your awareness. Give it some simple brief word or phrase that catches the essence of what you want to contemplate. For example, I might choose my anxiety about getting this work done, or a feeling of impatience that I have at the moment, or the beauty of a rose, or a spiritual image or name, or a situation that I'm finding challenging.

2. **Sustain a wordless contemplation** of what you have chosen

3. **Insight**: Allow a very subtle merging with what you chose and allow any insights or understandings to arise.

What we repeatedly contemplate bears fruit. It is very creative. However, it requires patience, a letting go, crucially without any expectation of a result, something many Westerners are not very used to doing. Sometimes you may need to contemplate something over a period of sessions for an awareness to come; and it might be that you get several awarenesses over time.

You will benefit from relaxing in one or more of the ways described in this chapter. So, first choose your topic or whatever, relax, and then give your topic a wordless contemplation. Any thoughts that arise -

just notice them and bring your attention back to the wordless contemplation. It may feel like a meditation, but this time you are holding your awareness on your chosen topic, *without thinking about it*. It is like it is just there in your mind's eye. You really are suspending any temptation to work it out. I imagine that is quite a challenge to the analysts amongst you, but worth it. You are also gently keeping your mind focused; it will probably want to wander off somewhere and, as with meditation, the art is to catch yourself doing this and bring your awareness back to your topic. Your subconscious is getting to work on it! What you have to do is to get out of the way, so to speak. A bit like life, in fact!

This is great training in awareness. With steady practice, you will slowly find your awareness getting sharper. Give it time.

Activity: Practising awareness

Something you could do every day as and when you have time to yourself is to give some time to simply being aware of what is happening moment by moment.

For example, as you walk to catch a train, bus or tube, simply allow yourself to be aware of walking, one foot in front of the other, the path you are walking on, what is around you, the people you see, the buildings, the cars or the vegetation. Notice how you are feeling, notice any body sensations, notice the air and notice how it feels as you breathe air in and out. Notice any thoughts and then put them to one side while you return your awareness to just being aware. Every time you start going off on some train of thought, just notice that and come back to being aware.

This process naturally brings us to the topic of meditation, which is not dissimilar.

Meditation

Meditation is one way to develop both a greater knowledge of your centred, contented Self that is being described in this book, and also to be more aware of how your ego works, when it is present and how to let it go.

You do not need to be an adherent of some religion or spiritual practice in order to meditate. It is simply a practice. Like so many of the techniques we have been exploring, it is quite simple to do but needs regular practice and persistence to get the benefit.

Activity: meditation

Find a quiet place where you will not be disturbed. You will need an upright chair to sit on that is reasonably comfortable, perhaps with a cushion to support your lower back. Or you can always adopt a crossed-leg or a lotus posture if you are supple enough. The lotus posture is used a lot in the East, as in Yoga, and is a particular cross-legged position.

People who meditate regularly like to create a special place for meditation, and may set aside a room or a part of a room for this purpose.

Sit with an upright posture; this is where you might need the cushion to support your lower back. Place your hands on your lap, with the palms facing upwards, one on top of the other, or with your palms lying downwards with one hand on each thigh. Make yourself comfortable by adjusting your posture a bit. You might also adjust your posture if you can so that your back is comfortably straight.

Look ahead inside, perhaps with the eyes a bit lowered. Close your eyes. Allow your awareness to start to go inside.

Take a few deep breaths, breathing in through your nose and so that you inflate your belly, pushing the diaphragm downwards. Imagine you are breathing into your belly. As you breathe out, allow yourself

Becoming aware

to relax. As you breathe in again, imagine you are breathing into any areas of tension in your body and as you breathe out you are letting the tension go.

With each breath, which is by now getting less deep and more rhythmical, you might find an increasing calm within you. Enjoy this calm. Welcome it in.

Allow yourself to notice your breath coming in, gently paying attention to the sensation of the breath as it passes through the nostrils, through the nasal passages, down the throat and into your lungs. And notice each sensation as you breathe out

You could spend your meditation just watching your breath and enjoying your state of calm. Notice too your easy feelings as they grow within you.

If any thoughts come to mind, just notice them and have the intention that they will pass by of their own accord, like clouds in the sky. Don't get into a train of thought. Stay detached and notice them, like you were noticing your breath. And return your attention to your breath. If you find you've been wrapped up in thought, just say to yourself "There go those thoughts again", accept it, and return your attention to your breath.

After a little while, take several deeper breaths and very gently start to bring your awareness back to the room and when you are ready, open your eyes. You might meditate for say 10 minutes at first but try to extend it to 20 minutes or half an hour with practice.

Experienced meditators will meditate for longer. What is more important is to develop a regular practice, so that you start to notice the benefits. Also mediators use other ways to have a focus as well as the breath. One such tool is a mantra, a group of Sanskrit words with a special meaning, like "*So 'ham*" meaning "I am That", but there are Western words one might use just as well like "Peace".

Meditation

As a tool for self-awareness

What comes up in meditation is always valuable, even if it does not seem like it. Even meditations that are full of thoughts are also still valuable. The idea is to learn to be unattached to your thoughts, to let them go and to allow them to subside into the background. Meditation is best practised over time, on a regular daily basis, so that you can train yourself to focus your mind.

When you are feeling a lot, or there's a lot going on for you and your ego is hard at it, meditation is a great way of becoming more aware of what's getting to you and choicefully letting it go. Many would say that the whole idea of meditation is to become unattached to thoughts and feelings, to notice them, breathe them away and return your awareness to your focus, the breath or the mantra. By doing that, you can start to experience a deeper, calmer reality. People often find they get insights into what's been bothering them, not by thinking about them but by just letting them be, focusing on their practice and allowing any insight to arise just by itself.

For example, you might start your meditation by asking yourself what you need to understand, such as an answer to something that is bothering you. Then let it go and go into meditation. Then at the end, see what's there for you. You might get an answer, but don't be attached to whether you get it or not. It's all about letting go.

Knowing more of yourself

With practice and with a bit longer in meditation, what happens is that the mind goes quiet all by itself. It is said, "A watched mind becomes still". Then you can start to enjoy the sense of calm and peace and the growing sense of contentment and then maybe the growing sense of affection, joy, love or whatever is your experience as your contentment wells up. And then you start to get to know, bit by bit, who you really are.

The art then is to carry that growing awareness into your life in the world. There too you can notice what comes up, not be attached to it,

Becoming aware

let it go and return your awareness to your contented self. Meditation is a way of training the mind to support your real self and not the ego.

Books on meditation, and teachers of meditation, are legion. Here are some:

Jack Kornfield, *Meditation for Beginners*, New York, Bantam, New York, 1993: a very good introduction, very accessible. Sogyal Rinpoche, *Meditation: a little book of wisdom*, San Francisco, Rider, 1994, taken from his bigger book, *The Tibetan Book of Living and Dying*: it is a short book and fits in a pocket or handbag. Both are Buddhist approaches.

Swami Muktananda, *Meditate*, Albany, SYDA Foundation, 1980: an Indian guru. Swami Durgananda, *The Heart of Meditation*, South Fallsburg, SYDA Foundation, 2002 (she is now called Sally Kempton): a wonderful, subtle and detailed exploration of the art of meditation. Both are from the Hindu yoga tradition.

The present moment

Of course the key point about all this is that when we are aware, we can start to do something about it, maybe to change it or whatever else we need to do to put ourselves back on track. However, before that happens there are some other key aspects to be aware of in the process. Most of us like to jump into action to fix something, when often it can work better if we go step by step through the awareness process.

The point of awareness is a "now" event

Awareness is something that occurs "right now". In some way, we become aware of something and in doing so it brings us right into the present.

Let's say you are walking down the road absorbed in some train of thought and then suddenly you noticed that actually it is a brilliantly beautiful sunny afternoon with not a cloud in the sky and the birds are singing like they are celebrating. You just became aware of your surroundings, you became "in the moment" as we say.

When we become aware of the present moment, we may experience an alertness, a heightened sense of reality. Other things that had been preoccupying us fade into the background. People talk of "aha" moments, maybe sudden realisations. They suddenly illumine the situation or move it on in some way. Feelings may flood in as a result, positive or otherwise or there may be excitement and a sense of new possibility. Or they may just feel very still and calm.

The point about "now" is that it is, in a sense, always there. We just need to bring it to our attention.

Activity: the "now"

So, right now, as you are reading this, stop, breathe in more deeply and, very gently and slowly, just notice the breath coming in and going out. Just *feel* the sensation of the breath on your nostrils, in your nasal passages, in your throat, going down into your lungs, the movement of your chest and diaphragm.....Now become aware of the moment....like you are looking at it...not thinking, just looking, breathing and waiting....like a cat waiting for a mouse....intently focused on the moment......Stay like that for a few moments....And then breathe again and come back.

Note down anything you noticed
....
....
....
....
....
....

People often say they experience a quite different sense of themselves when they first start to focus on the present moment.

Eckhart Tolle says that in being very focused on the present moment all else falls away[5]. He says that the "Now" has great potential for insight, opening portals to a heightened sense of reality and to higher realities, as well as opening opportunities for making a difference for ourselves. We might say that the only thing that exists is the present moment. What happened in the past is just that, it has passed, and no longer exists. In each moment there is another possibility, perhaps many possibilities. Each possibility coexists with the others, and depending on how you choose, many other things are possible. You can thus recreate each moment anew.

Pause and become present

So, we do just that, pause.....and attend to the present moment. And be right there, in the moment.

It is as simple, as obvious and as natural as that. Let go of your thoughts. Just allow the awareness of the moment to be there. As

---

[5] Eckhart Tolle, *The Power of Now*, London, Hodder and Stoughton, 2001

before, take a deep breath to help you if you need to. Breathing is a very "now" activity. We've been doing it all our lives. Focusing on the act of breathing takes our awareness away from what has been preoccupying us, and the out-breath is relaxing and helps us to let go. So, we breathe in deeply and become aware of the moment. We breathe out what is bothering us, letting go.

Of course we can then notice what we've been up to mentally and here's the chance to check it out. In doing this we have taken the capacity to detach ourselves from our on-going stream of thoughts and to tap into a much deeper source of power, **Witness Consciousness**.

Witnessing your mental stream

There is another part of us that is aware of ourselves as we sense, feel, think and act. It has been described as the part of us that is "already always knowing". Meditators in the eastern tradition have experienced the sense within us that there is a one who watches us as we think. This part of us is not judging. Contrary to widely held belief, the "inner judge" or "inner critic" is another form of ego. The part I am referring to just notices. Hence we describe this part as the Witness.

You might notice the Witness yourself as you catch yourself doing something that you aren't comfortable with or you realise isn't serving you. It might occur as you simply go about your everyday activities. It's that part that lies in the background, simply knowing and aware.

When we pause and come into the present moment, we also potentially tap into the Witness part of ourselves. From that place, we can just notice what we're doing, potentially let it go and move on. In being in the moment we've become still. We are very possibly no longer caught up in our stuff. We catch ourselves, see it is not serving us and drop it. The Witness space enables us to SEE IT. This is why it has such power for change.

This way of perceiving human potential has great possibility; for many it has proved revolutionary in their lives. It is also ultimately perfectly simple. As I said, just get it, drop it and move on.

Becoming aware

One might say, "But it is not really as simple as that", and it isn't for those very many of us who have spent most of their lives caught up in knee-jerk thinking, in compulsiveness, where our patterns of feeling, thinking and behaving have got us in their grip, where we remain stuck. We will look more at that when we explore the mind in Part Two. For such people, it takes lots of practice over time to unlearn these habits. And it can be done. Witnessing is a crucial step. Here we interrupt the stream of thinking, pause, be still, see what we're doing to ourselves and have the opportunity to stop. The pattern may re-occur, and probably will, but the more we see what we're doing and check it, the more we are stopping old habits and enabling the learning of new habits.

A familiar example

Let's take a very well-known example, one that most of us probably experience quite a few times: You are travelling to work. You got held up at home and now you're behind. The traffic is worse than usual. It's wet and people are driving more slowly. The queues are building up. You look at your clock and start to get anxious, or maybe irritable with the others in front of you. If only they had better road sense and would drive this way rather than that, you'd get to work on time. As it is, you're afraid you'll be late. So you start to feel guilty. You start to have imaginary conversations with your boss about what he or she will say. You get more and more tense and the delays seem to get worse. And then….lo and behold….you catch yourself giving yourself and the rest of the world an incredibly hard time. You pause, breathe, let go of the angst, and say to yourself, "There I go again, beating myself up….I'll stop that right now….I surrender". You breathe away the angst, give up all that really very useless thinking, put on a nice, relaxing piece of music and just be in the moment. And then….somehow the traffic eases and you get there right on time, feeling OK. You might even reflect ruefully, why did I give myself such a hard time? It was OK after all!

What happened is, as I said, very simple. You very probably do it in other ways already. You caught yourself repeating your pattern (we've left out the detail), and made the choice to stop. Your Witness self has enabled you to seize control of the moment. In the moment of Now, you exercised a different choice. Previous witnessing has already identified your tendency to beat yourself and others up in certain situations. The more you spot it, the more you give yourself power to drop it, to give it up. It really doesn't serve you and you don't need it.

Is it useful?

In assessing something that we have witnessed, we ask ourselves this simple but powerful question, "Is it useful?" Traditionally we might ask if this is "right or wrong". But to do that is to place a judgement on our behaviour, usually one that we have taken on from other people earlier on in our life, in particular our parents. It can come as quite a shock to discover that we govern our behaviour through other people's rules. Some refer to it as the "inner critic", which has replaced an earlier external critic. We adopt, sometimes unquestioningly, societal, religious or parental rules and then judge ourselves by that. This might have served to take care of us at some time. But it may now be outmoded.

A far simpler approach is to ask if it is useful to us *now*. If it is of value, then continue with it, if not discard it for something more satisfying.

For example, on a workshop a timid man had started to express how he felt in forceful terms, such that we lauded his authenticity and power in asserting himself at long last. However, he ended each assertion with a quiet "I'm sorry", which quite undermined what he had said. He was not aware he was doing it. When others pointed it out, he realised that that is what he had said to his parents and later in life he had continued like this. He had felt very guilty whenever he had expressed his needs. He could now choose to let go of what he no longer needed. He saw that it did not serve him.

Tips for anchoring your awareness in the "Now"

Here is a range of ways of accessing the present, some summarising what we've covered before.

i. Meditation

Meditation is a state of relaxed alertness, where attention is focused on the present. It is recommended that you have at least one period of meditation a day, of at least 20 minutes, and preferably two. Ideally be free from interruption.

Sit in an upright posture. Go through an initial process of deep breathing and relaxation and then focus on the ***breath***. Become a detached observer of your thoughts and simply allow them to be there. Gradually thinking subsides and is replaced by an awareness of the present moment. Stay present like this. If thoughts come, just notice them but choose not to follow them. Just let them be. Thoughts can become like clouds passing in the sky. You notice them and let them go. Bring your awareness back to your breathing and awareness of the Now. A variation is to repeat a mantra. It is said that repeating a mantra bores the ego to death. Contemplative prayer can be similar.

ii. Tuning into the body

Tune into your body, taking your attention within. Relax, using the breath to guide you within. Become focused on the ***felt sense*** of the body and its invisible energy field. Imagine your mind's eye, inside your body, scanning one part and then another part. Allow yourself to **feel** that part of your body. Let go of any thoughts and emotions. Become still and observant. Really become alert to the inner sense of that part of your body.

This body awareness is a means of anchoring yourself in the Now. It is a way of re-connecting yourself. If you keep some of your awareness in your body while engaged in everyday activities, it can be a means of maintaining that anchor. A particularly powerful process is to lie down and, step by step, flood each part of your body with awareness energy and let the whole body be alive with energy for a short while.

The present moment

iii. The now

Deliberately focus on the present moment. Become very alert to the moment. Free yourself from thinking by becoming the **Witness** of the mind and watching the mind. It is said, "A watched mind becomes still". The one who watches is the deeper self. In the stream of thinking there is often a *Gap*, where you can pause and enter the present. Just stay still and observe it. If your mind strays, become aware of that and, without judgement, shift attention back to the now.

Meditators use the gap in breathing to take them deeper into meditation. They focus on the pauses between breaths.

iv. Surrender

This is the process of letting go or giving up emotional-mental resistance to the flow of the moment and is a discipline often related to the above activities. This release is often experienced as a lightening up and brings a rush of contentment. Letting go our personal baggage is therefore key.

v. Silence

Inner silence can be attained even in the noisiest places. It becomes possible to be silent and still even when you are on a busy, noisy train. Pause, breathe, and take your awareness within. Become very aware. Allow your thoughts to gradually still themselves.

vi. Pausing

Before thinking, speaking and acting, it can be helpful to briefly pause and go within. You re-connect yourself with your life-force.

vii. Pure awareness

Here you stop and become intensely aware of what is. This is particularly powerful in noticing surroundings, as with being in nature, but it is also very effective in being aware of people.

Taking responsibility

Once we come into the "now", we can then let go of what's not working, what does not serve us, and return to a stable state of mind. It is crucial to mark this step in understanding the potential that we humans have for making a difference for ourselves.

This is a very important moment in developing our ability to manage our lives in ways that really work for us. What we are doing at this point is taking control of our process. This is an act of will. What we need to do in personal growth is to build up our will, our ability to make choices. In current parlance, part of this is referred to as "taking responsibility" or "being accountable" to yourself.

Responsibility is response-ability

In taking responsibility, what happens is that we make a decision: "I am responsible for my life and the decisions I make". What this means is we take ownership. What we are potentially saying here is that "As a human being I create what occurs in my life".

This can be a challenging statement to make, especially as for many it seems to fly in the face of their reality. To them, others or circumstances have caused what occurs and they can cite many concrete examples to support this.

We are creatures who have learned to interpret the world according to our perceptions. From childhood we learned that things happen to us. We think we don't have control; others do. So, what occurs seems to confirm this experience. We become victims of life. And the world has a way of showing up as we think. So we get it in our lives. What we need to do is change our perception and this experience changes.

Viktor Frankl was a survivor of the notorious prison camp of Auschwitz under the Nazis. In *Man's Search for Meaning* he described the enormous suffering of himself and his fellow inmates. What he learned was that those that survived starvation and disease until liberation exercised a spiritual freedom, a choice to choose one's

Taking responsibility

attitude, to stay alive and make meaning in an apparently meaningless situation. They were not, he wrote, responsible for how they got there but they were responsible for how they dealt with it. Those who lost their purpose and sense of meaning literally gave up and died[6].

One of the founders of Gestalt Therapy, Fritz Perls, said that in taking responsibility we take "response-ability": we develop the ability to respond to our inner awareness. In Gestalt therapy, the human organism makes its choices based on its sensing and awareness, from which mobilisation and action flow.

Let's take an example from the world of relationships. It might be that when your partner is feeling uptight or upset he or she has a knack of speaking quite sharply to you. You might feel angry and in turn react sharply and speak angrily. Sounds familiar? This is a common way that rows start. It might seem as if your partner has "caused" your anger, that he or she is responsible. However, from a personal development perspective neither is responsible for the other's feelings. We each are responsible for our own. It is us ourselves who feel the feelings. Feelings can be our warning sign, telling us something we need to attend to. However, very often they are also learned behaviour. It is possible, in our example, that you had a parent who spoke sharply with you and you had a reaction to it. So your partner is triggering a memory. Your partner might be very effectively and unintentionally pushing your buttons of past unfinished business. We sometimes speak of reaction as "re-action", a repeat of a past action. If each took responsibility for his or her own feelings in a situation, we wouldn't then blame the other in some way for the upset.

Activity: Taking responsibility

Now take some time to reflect, really reflect. Be honest with yourself: In which areas of your life do you take responsibility?
....
....

---

[6] Viktor Frankl, *Man's Search for Meaning,* English edition, New York, Pocket Books, 1959, p. 98.

And in which areas do you not take responsibility?

....
....
....
....
....
....

It is very subtle how we can opt out of responsibility in some areas and yet be fully responsible in others. Very often we flip from one polarity to another, in one situation being very much "in control" and then, say, start sounding off on how badly we're being dealt with by others in another situation. So, review what you've written and see where you are avoiding applying responsibility. This is often where we are reluctant to fully face up to a behaviour of ours and deal with it.

Honesty

In some cases, after witnessing and before you take responsibility for what you do, you may need first to acknowledge to yourself that that behaviour is yours. You may need to be honest with yourself: "Yes, I do that". This can be particularly difficult if someone has pointed it out and you resist taking ownership, or if you have a particularly strong inner critic. It may feel like swallowing your pride, admitting you were "wrong", were "at fault", have been "found out", that others "see it", and so on – all this is the ego at work. Admitting even to yourself that that is how you've been all this time, can put you in touch with a part of your limited self, your ego, that feels "not good enough" or "unworthy" or "ashamed".

Taking responsibility

In personal growth, it helps to cultivate honesty, even **humility**. You've not really done anything "wrong". At another level after all, it "just is", something that happens. All the rest are your ego judgements at work. More of this later.

Choosing your reality

We create our own reality

Once we take responsibility and exercise choice, we are exercising real control over our lives. Then we can start to create anew. This brings us again to the point made above that we are highly creative, more so than we often realise. We create our own reality. It therefore follows that we can choose again and create something different. As a result we can change our experience. This process is well described in *The Law of Attraction* by Esther and Jerry Hicks[7].

What is critical here is that we start with a clear idea of what we are intending to create and stick with it. An example that is often given in this regard is how people will report having had either a good or bad day based on how they started the day thinking how the day was going to be. This is also referred to as the self-fulfilling prophecy. How you see a certain situation at the start may as a result be what you get. Looking at this positively, many people report how if they envisage a car park space being available a few minutes before arriving they usually get one. I am often struck how, if I estimate a time of arrival and a length of time I think a journey will take, what happens usually turns out to be what I'd envisaged.

The beliefs we choose and the part they play

It is often said that people create their own heaven or hell. In the psychology called Transactional Analysis, it is said that a person's life will unfold according to their "life script", the decisions they had made about life based on their early experiences. Let us say that a small child decided that, as a result of an early formative experience he was unlovable, he would then create life experiences where he would get to feel people don't like him. Or a person behaves in a repeatedly unpleasant way to dear ones or repeatedly meets unpleasant people in her life, because she made an early decision that "I'm bad".

---

[7] Esther and Jerry Hicks, *The Law of Attraction*, Carlsbad, CA, Hay House, 2008

Choosing your reality

Perhaps this was because she was told when very small that she was "bad" or concluded from what happened that this must be because she was "bad".

The point to be made here is that this is emphatically not who we are. But this might be who we think we are. We make up beliefs about ourselves, life, other people, situations, and so on. And we live life out of those beliefs. We are not usually aware of what those beliefs are. They sometimes take a bit of unpicking.

Crucially, we can change our beliefs and make up new ones that serve us. One particular Western philosophy, Existentialism has as one of its core concepts that since life is in itself meaningless, we can choose our own meaning.

We can change our experience

So, we can choose a new set of experiences. Take care what you choose, because this is powerful stuff. A well-known example is the practice where people envision and write down a description of the new partner they would like to create in their life. It is a very powerful technique and many people say it actually works! You might like to try it. Just be careful however that you get the description exactly as you want though, because I've also met people who have got one element not quite as they really intended, or missed something out, and then created someone who didn't really work out as they wanted. For example someone might write down that they want someone who is "available" but since they are not being specific enough might draw to themselves one who is married!

Another example might be the person who thought she was bad. Let us say that she decided that she was not going to see herself like that anymore but would instead say to herself that she was a good person, a radiant being of light, and that she would henceforth love herself come what may. Initially she may be challenged by this, as we usually get tested one way or the other. An inner voice may say, "No you're not like that - you're bad", and she would have to counter that by persisting with her new beliefs. Then she might meet people who treat her badly and she would need to firmly assert herself from her "good" space. Then, while that may pass, she might still meet people who treat others badly, and so on. In time, these experiences will be replaced by ones where people experience her as a lovely person and she comes to change her understanding of herself at her core and to know the beauty inside her and around her. The world we experience is the outcome of our view about it.

This is the really potent healing that is possible once we choose to change our negative self-perceptions. How we feel about ourselves and what world we experience can profoundly change for the better. Just think how much of the world is made up of people with negative self-beliefs!

Neale Donald Walsch in his powerful dialogue with God described in *Conversations with God*,[8] quotes God as saying that we always have the chance to create anew. He stressed that we create by thought, word and deed. He calls these the three tools of creation. We therefore need to attend to our intentions in all three areas and to closely monitor our thoughts, words and actions to be consistent with what we intend.

In a later book, *Friendship with God*[9] Walsch, quoting God again, goes on to say that one can go a step further by shifting your state of being before something happens and get a wholly more beneficial result. Getting in touch with her "good" self before she makes contact with people, would be an example of how our person mentioned above would be able to impact positively the difficult people she might be interacting with. What she would be doing is shifting her inner state. This is the power of mastery, when we are able at will to step into our centred state and not be affected by our stuff or that of others. This is when we truly start to realise our inner power for good.

---

[8] Neale Donald Walsch, *Conversations with God, Book One*, London (UK edition), Hodder & Stoughton, 1997
[9] Neale Donald Walsch, *Friendship with God*, London (UK Edition), Hodder and Stoughton, 1999

The difference between believing and knowing

There is, however, a step beyond choosing beliefs, and that is when we just know. Most humans live their lives out of their perceptions based on their life experiences. These are dysfunctional. They do not serve us. They fail the fundamental test of usefulness. There is another level, that of knowledge. Knowledge in this sense is an inner truth; it just is. This is when all systems, constructs and beliefs fall away because we have contacted at a profound level who we really are. Here we know ourselves as beings of joy, bliss, love, fun, laughter, compassion and all the good things that we know about but have difficulty in consistently being in touch with. As highly developed people in all the main spiritual traditions have shown, when we do contact our inner truth, we just know. It has a kind of enduring joy about it, a welling up again and again of a loving that knows no bounds and is not attached to any particular person. There is no doctrine here, no belief system, nothing you have to sign up to, just an inner contentment, a purity of being.

Until we get there, we still do know, albeit in fits and starts. It sits around, on the edge of our experience. We talk about it, for a start. People write about it. One of the benefits of this path is that more and more, as we strip away the layers of our "egos", we come to know what this knowing is.

Being aware

In all this, the key is **self-awareness**: the more you understand and know what disturbs your equilibrium, where your thoughts go, what comes up for you, what your patterns are, what upsets you, and what gets you going, the more you can manage it. Once you understand yourself, then you can apply the skills of awareness to master and let go of these disruptive aspects of what is essentially your "ego self", not who you really are.

In this book we also focus a lot on the art of **letting go**. Once you are aware of what you do, you can take responsibility for what comes up, choose to do things differently and then intentionally let go of what does not serve you. Really this requires practice, such that you can even get to the point where you can just drop whatever is going on for you. Here you are getting close to mastery, where you know what's happening, where you can see that it's not who you are and you have developed mental and emotional "muscle" so that you know how to let something go – and then you just drop it, just like that.

Let's be clear. This takes lots of practice. But it can be done. What is key is to develop the self-awareness so that you know what is coming up and you can exercise the steps described above so that you can begin to let go. The next part is now devoted to helping understand more about what comes up for you and how you can manage it.

Part 2: Is this who you really are?

Is this who you really are?

Managing your mind

So often people I work with ask about how they can manage the "internal chatter" that goes on in their minds, the persistent thoughts and feelings that they would rather not have. So much of today's lifestyle is taken up with what I call addictive behaviour, activities to divert our attention from what our minds get up to. Smoking, alcohol and drugs are the bane of our so-called civilisation. I meet people who are trying to give up smoking or drink but then eat more to compensate, such do they want to avoid having to face themselves. The malaise is rampant.

Yet it doesn't have to be this way, if only we addressed the real issues. It doesn't have to mean years of therapy. For the vast majority of us, it is a matter of attending to what our minds do and training ourselves to do it differently. The ancient sages of India understood this and taught their disciples to use technique to so manage the mind that in time they could at will centre their minds in a steady state of equipoise, where mental unease would not disturb them. This involved meditative technique but also an understanding of how the mind worked. To do that, they undertook self-enquiry.

So in this part, we will also explore self-enquiry, in a modern western way but with the same objective, going further into understanding and managing those thoughts and feelings that take us off-track. Then you can more effectively manage your mind so that these thoughts and feelings no longer pull you off-track. Then you can live a more centred, purposeful and contented life.

In doing this, you will as we have seen be using awareness – noticing what is going on. Now we will focus on what that awareness can reveal, and how you might manage it.

This sometimes means being ready to look at your personal demons, so to speak. It would be no surprise if you said you really don't like to go there, but it can be your route to fulfilment. What you **resist** is well worth looking at, since it probably contains clues for your ultimate success. "What you resist, you get". What you resist, or fight against or try not to allow to come up, will usually get magnified and get in the way for you even more. So you perhaps do need to deal with it.

Is this who you really are?

What you think, you are

The mind is often perceived as an obstacle. Yet it is a big ally in our growth. We simply need to find a way to make it work for our higher interest. It helps to know the tricks it gets up to and through self-awareness we can start to move beyond the limitations it can create.

What is "the mind"?

The term "mind" is used in various senses. These include the following:

 i. A collection of mental processes and acts
 ii. The totality of the conscious and unconscious mental experiences of an individual
 iii. Equivalent to the brain
 iv. Intelligence
 v. A characteristic or trait

This book will tend to use the second sense. Recent research has suggested that the mind is something that exists beyond the brain. Scientists now consider it includes the whole body given what is now known about the sensitivities of the individual cell membrane[10]. Some even say that it also exists beyond the body. It uses the brain as an instrument. In the mind is the totality of our experiences. It is where our senses and feelings, thoughts and perceptions are interpreted and where thoughts occur in which we make meaning.

Who we think we are is the totality of these past experiences, made sense of again in the present moment when we think a thought. However as explored in Part 1, our minds have far greater potential. Our task is to harness it for our own well-being and higher purpose.

---

[10] Bruce Lipton, *The Biology of Belief*, Carlsbad, CA, Hay House, 2008

What we believe manifests in our lives

What we think, we become. We create our own reality: we are hugely creative. We can use our minds to create something we wish to happen for our own good. However, we do not see ourselves as such. We see ourselves as limited; such is how the Ego works.

It can be useful to see how our ideas about ourselves show up in our lives. In other words, things that happen might relate to ideas I might have about me. For example, if I see myself as hard-working, while I might see that as a virtue what I might get in my life is a lot of hard work! Now, that might be OK, but it might be worth exploring whether this idea always serves me. I might in the long run be getting something that is not what I really need.

At a more fundamental level we hold beliefs about ourselves, other people and circumstances that can govern our reality.

    a. A person might believe she cannot sing. Now this might be because she decided that in music classes at school. Maybe she decided when she was a lot smaller that she was "not good enough". So that decision affected how she perceived her ability at things she was learning. Therefore when she attempts to sing she sounds flat and out of tune. The belief is reinforced and she then avoids music in her life. Only in later life does she take singing lessons and discovers she has a beautiful contralto voice.

    b. Another person believes that "money is the root of all evil". Let's say he grew up in a household that thought that. So he experiences lack of money. When he gets it, he never seems to be able to hold on to it. Also he finds that he has bad experiences around money. People seem to cheat him of it. Bad experiences seem always to be money-related. No wonder that he finds it so challenging to learn about creating wealth and abundance in his life. They cut across his underlying belief.

Is this who you really are?

These underlying beliefs may be described as **root thoughts**, core to our thinking and therefore to what occurs in our lives, to what we create.

Activity: How do your root thoughts show up in your life?

As an experiment, write down all the statements that you believe describe you, starting each time with "I am…" For example I might write, "I am hard-working; I am gentle; I am irritable".

....
....
....
....
....
....
....

Which of these might be "root thoughts"? For example, where has this thought governed how you have lived your life for many years, maybe one you grew up with?

....
....
....
....
....
....
....

When you've finished, look at each statement: do they relate to what happens in your life (eg. Situations that occur, events that happen, relationships, work, etc)?

....
....
....
....

Now write down the things you notice that do actually happen, positive or negative. For example, if I write that I am hard-working, I think of times when I've been so.

The point is that we can use our minds to change these underlying thoughts and beliefs. With self-awareness we can catch ourselves using these thoughts and then we can put other, more empowering ones in their place.

We can choose our own preferred reality

Moment by moment we can intentionally start to use different thoughts that can create different outcomes. We can also use the mind to help us identify when the limited, small self, the Ego is at work and we can therefore learn to challenge its negativity. We can even learn to be in such a space that we can be unattached to the egoic behaviours of our mind and enter a calm, centred place of equilibrium. For example, you may choose to think that who you are is a source of peace and calm. You would need to work on your thoughts so that you feel more calm and peaceful but also work to perceive the world "out there" as peaceful and calm – even if, for the moment, it doesn't seem that way. Remember, this is a perception we've created.

Is this who you think you are?

You are not your Past

Who we believe we are is the product of past experience, usually acquired over a life-time. Many of us are prisoners of this past. But it is not who we are

How we learned all this stuff

Most of us learn about life from our parents, immediate family, friends and peers, school and work, usually in that order. Usually one's psychological make-up is all in place by the age of 7 and what follows builds on that basic structure. The thing about being below the age of 7 is that our ability to understand, choose and discriminate was very limited. We made decisions about ourselves, other people and life based often on inaccurate information. One of the classic examples of this is that, if parents rowed seriously or split up, children often blamed themselves. Then in later life they might have a problem of commitment to relationships. Thus major events in the family in a child's early years often have a formative impact on their personality.

Parent and child styles in adulthood

What we learned as children can show up in adulthood. Here is an example from psychology.

In Transactional Analysis, originated by Eric Berne, it is said that adults can switch their behaviour between 3 modes, or "ego states", parent, adult and child. The Adult behaviour would be where we operate in a stable manner, unattached to egoic ways. In the Parent mode, we can be either nurturing or critical. The nurturing mode would be supportive and encouraging, for example. The critical style would probably be where you might be giving someone else a hard time. In the Child mode, we can be the free child, or we can be the rebel, the compliant or the withdrawn one. The free child is spontaneous, fun-loving, or natural. The other three styles probably speak for themselves. An example of when the ego might be working is where a woman might be in the critical parent style at home with her partner, sharply pointing out what he hasn't done very well in the house, and yet that same person at work might be the compliant child with her boss, responding obediently to his demands even though she isn't happy with them[11].

The point is that we learned this stuff as children and we continue to act it out in adulthood with each other.

It influences our perceptions of the world and ourselves

As children, we made some pretty crucial decisions about life. We saw in the last section how the woman who believed she could not sing had probably decided early on that she was "not good enough".

What decisions did you make?

Activity: Decisions about life

> It might be useful for you to reflect on what decisions you made when you were small. Think back on your life and go back to your earliest memories. Which ones really stick in your mind? Where do these events relate to you, or about your view of yourself, or to you in relation to your parents, or about your parents, or about other people, or about what life was like? What decisions did you make?
>
> ....
> ....
> ....
> ....
> ....
> ....
> ....
> ....
> ....

---

[11] Eric Berne, *Games People Play: The Psychology of Human Relationships*, New York, Balantine Books, 1964. Thomas Harris, *I'm OK-You're OK*, New York, Avon books, 1996

Is this who you really are?

Generally we can each come up with at least one or two fairly basic ones.

Then ask yourself what impact those decisions have had on your life since.

....
....
....
....
....
....
....
....
....

Sometimes, we can uncover some uncomfortable insights in this way. However, there are also some major clues here for your path.

You are not your past

The key point at this stage is that we are not our past. This is not who we are. The great Self, beyond the Ego, is one of fun, joy, enjoyment, laughter, spontaneity, aliveness, bliss, and love. When we step into the great Self, the ego stuff falls away. Remember that what we need to do is be aware of what we no longer need, and then learn to let it go. This is one way of doing that.

What we are covering so far can also be applied to later formative events in our lives. You could ask yourself what behaviours you have adopted in the past that you now do not need.

Activity: Decisions to give up

Write down any that come to mind:
....
....
....
....
....

You are not your past

The past is just that, over and done with. It no longer exists. It is only that we allow ourselves to be prisoners of it.

We can change what we have grown up with

It is easy to stay stuck in the past. We can remain attached to our memories. A classic example is resentment or bitterness against one you are or were close to. People hold on to resentment against one or both of their parents or siblings and find it difficult to forgive. The memory keeps coming back, with all its attendant feelings. It can be hugely painful. This pain cannot be denied, especially where abuse and neglect were involved. The effects on some people's lives can be devastating. Yet from the growth point of view, no one benefits from holding on to past pain and we need to find a way to give it up. Such holding on is an example of the **blame game**. It is common among people as they grow up and tends to continue in adulthood: "Other people are responsible for what has happened to me and they are to blame". We carry on with the blame game as adults with people who come into our lives, especially at work and in relationships, and this is an excellent example of not taking responsibility.

The optimistic possibility is that we can change this. What we do henceforth is down to us. For you, the reader, this may be a very good moment to start. As explained in the part about taking responsibility, we need to catch what we do that is not useful, take responsibility for it and then work to let it go. For deep-seated issues, this can take time and effort, but it can be done.

We chose this life to learn what we needed to learn

One further, extraordinary-seeming possibility is that we chose what we experienced in order to learn what we needed to learn in this lifetime. This is not necessarily obvious. Yet our experiences are also

Is this who you really are?

gifts for us in some way. As my wife says, "Every problem has a gift for you in its hands"[12].

When people look back over their past experiences, when they can see beyond what troubled them, they find that they have been equipped or served in some way. A single child may have regretted aspects of her childhood where she had no one to play with and at times felt lonely or left to her own devices. Yet she may in later life have found that her ability to use her own resources, to be self-reliant and have an independence of spirit, served her well in her career and in the challenges she faced. Also she may have decided that she would have more than one child.

Our parents in particular probably did their best, knowing what they knew and equipped with what they had. Looking beyond blame, what could you thank them for that they have taught you? You could extend this to include other significant people in your life.

Activity: Gratitude exercise

What could you thank someone else for that they have taught you or given you, intentionally or otherwise?
....
....
....
....
....
....
....

As a follow-up, how about now going and thanking them? It can be very healing for you and it could be a gift for someone else.

Expressing gratitude for what we have, both tangible and intangible, is a hugely valuable activity. It is especially useful when we think we are lacking in certain things, like money, a job, or well-being. When done

---

[12] Perry Akasha Lonsdale, *How to do Life*, Wiltshire, UK, EP Books, 2004, p. 54.

authentically there is an honouring in the process, a giving to others or to Life itself, from the heart. In fact it helps open the heart. In the process we get to see what we truly have. We come to see ourselves to be truly blessed for what we actually have. Many of us are so wrapped up in thinking we lack things that we fail to acknowledge what we do have. Expressing gratitude can take us to a place where we can appreciate the value of things that are basic to our lives, like love, the company of loved ones, humour, nature, the air we breathe, the sun that shines, the birds that sing, or Life itself. When people really work on letting go of the stuff that isn't working in their lives, they often come back to these basics. When we connect with who we really are, we rejoice in these things.

Perception

As humans, we interpret our world. We put it through our unique filtering system. That filtering system was developed as we've seen, over a lifetime and is based on our past experiences and our egos. Different people have different perceptions based on their own life experiences. Yet, beyond the different perceptions, there is an underlying commonality.

Interpretations: what we've made the world mean

It is like wearing a pair of coloured glasses, through which we see the world. Also other people have different colours in their glasses prescription.

An example

As a couple walked down a shopping street, the woman was indignant to see someone put a piece of rubbish in a flower-holder on the pavement. "Why," she exclaimed, "did that woman not put the paper in the rubbish bin over there?" There followed a brief discussion of the perceived habits of certain people in throwing rubbish on the road or pavement and not taking it home. The couple made these people thoroughly wrong. On reflection, one of the couple thought the woman did not look "the sort" who would do that, and also she was aware of how she very deliberately put the paper on the flower-holder. On returning past the flower holder later, they saw that the rubbish was in fact an envelope with someone's name on it facing upwards, and the envelope had been placed standing up so someone could see the name. They laughed, feeling a bit embarrassed, *"Interpretation!"* Maybe the woman had picked it up thinking that it had been dropped in error and had left it so that someone might be able to find it, perhaps an act of consideration.

A similar experience that people often report is that of first impressions. A person may not turn out to be as he first appeared. Yet, we might invent a whole story about this person before we get to know him, in which our own perceptions will play a major part. At

Perception

work, teams can be at war with each other because their managers do not see eye to eye. When the managers are brought together to sort this out, they start to see each other differently and in a better light. Each drops a perception he or she had about the other. Miraculously, the teams then get on great.

Activity: Your perceptions

What sort of negative perceptions of others do you frequently adopt at first sight?

....
....
....
....
....
....

We have interpreted the world based on this process. Things have happened in our lives and we have made them mean things which may not fit with the facts or as perceived by others. These events have gone through the filtering system of our egos. This was particularly likely in our childhood, when we were even less able to subject the process to objective analysis, or ask others to do so. But then, even in adulthood, does this objectivity exist? You may find those people that, in a subtle way, agree with your point of view and reinforce your perception. Whole groups can develop attitudes based on this approach.

From a personal growth standpoint, it is useful to remember that perceptions are just that, perceptions. What we experience may not be what others experience and what we experience is not who we are. We've made it all up.

Perception and knowledge

Behind our perceptions lie fundamental truths about us. The trouble is they are veiled, concealed from our awareness. Who we are is fun, laughter, aliveness, contentment, bliss, evenness of temperament,

Is this who you really are?

love, enjoyment, and the other qualities that we experience when we are in a centred state. Through self-awareness and managing our egos so that they do not disrupt our awareness, we can reveal that essential "us" more and more. That way, we find knowledge of who we are. With that, we also learn more about our world which, since it is a creation of our perception, starts to change too and reflects back to us who we truly are. If, for example we are filled with love, how can we not fill our world with love? The two go together, as many who have known love in their lives will testify. This "truth" is a truth to us, since we come to know it as true in our own eyes. This way, we find ultimate knowledge.

You can read more about interpretation in an excellent book, *"The Interpreted World"* by Ernesto Spinelli[13].

---

[13]Ernesto Spinelli, *The Interpreted World*, London, Sage, 1989

Feelings

Feelings are very useful: they alert us to things we need to be aware of. Very basically, emotions like fear are ways we have of avoiding danger. So in a positive sense they are very healthy.

Feelings are also the language of our soul. When we access our feelings we know what's really there, what is authentic. Such feelings touch others, who feel drawn to us and resonate with us. It is here that we can express what is deeply meaningful for us and can take us where we really want to go, to our heart's desire.

Yet certain uncomfortable feelings can disrupt our centred state. Very often these disruptive feelings are linked to thoughts. However, the impression is often that it is the feelings that we are most aware of. Since they are unpleasant, we learn to suppress them or avoid then by deflection. Yet they tend to stick around unless acknowledged and released.

Let's be clear. Feelings in themselves are just that, how you feel at any given moment. What naturally occurs is that the feeling just goes through our bodies and dissolves. Because we resist them and associate them with certain thoughts, they tend to stick around. We need to learn to healthily release them and let them dissolve themselves.

With self-awareness, we need to learn to identify the emotion and be able to discriminate between it and a balanced state. For example, you might enquire within and notice that a tightness in your stomach is a nagging anxiety, or the fact that your heart is beating faster is a rising anger inside.

Let's now look at a few: anger, sadness, fear, and love.

Anger

Anger can be useful. We can channel anger into action and making things happen. It's what is behind anger that is the question.

Is this who you really are?

We don't like anger because it has destructive connotations. People get hurt through anger, physically and mentally. It can boil up into a rage and we want to give vent to it in some way. Others won't feel safe around such a feeling. It is most obviously disruptive, not just for ourselves but for others too. More subtly, anger can take the form of irritability, grumpiness, underhandedness, sarcasm, resentment, and so on. It might explode at times, sparked by some trivial incident seemingly not much to do with the response, or it might just sit there in a silent fuming. Often it may seem to be directed against someone else.

Beneath anger, however, there is often pain. It is that which fuels the anger. We need to take responsibility for the feeling and also identify the pain underneath which fuels it.

Sadness

Tears may be tears of rage. They can be confused with sadness but are quite different. Sadness, if held on to, can lead to unhappiness and misery. The whole body energy sags. It is a contraction. The world closes in. One may become gloomy, sorrowful, and forlorn. Grief is one typical way it is experienced, when there has been a loss, although grief can contain other emotions too. Lack of love may be experienced as sadness, where one feels alone, abandoned even: "there is no one there for me". People are often searching for a partner to fill a hole inside themselves, an ultimately unfulfilling task since we can really only fill it with our own source of love and contentment.

Anger and sadness are often related to things in the past.

Fear

Fear is often described as the bottom-line emotion contrasted with love. Most disruptive feelings can be reduced to fear at some point. People who are on a path of personal growth will most likely hit fear at some point, often after a lot of work done on themselves. Often, it can be experienced as an anxiety, a **worry**, which can become repetitive, so much so that people develop a worry habit that they are in a sense attached to. This may need to lot of work to detach from. Fear may also manifest as nervousness. We may be reluctant to take on tasks for fear of the consequences. Fear can paralyse, so that we find it difficult to get things done.

Where fear can show up after a lot of personal growth work is in the form of an existential fear, a fear relating to existence, to being alive. People fear death, but are afraid to go there, so it is often unacknowledged. Yet, the fact is that we are going to die at some point and therefore at some point we need to confront this fact.

Another, even more fundamental aspect to fear is separation. This might be the fear of losing a loved one, or of not having a person to love in one's life. Behind that, some say, lies the experience of being separate from the whole, from humanity, from life, from the divine as one might understand it.

Fear is often present or future-related.

More complex feelings

Some feelings are more complex. The most obvious are guilt, shame, anxiety and depression. They usually contain a range of feelings inside them which have been described above.

Depression is depressed emotion, feelings not being surfaced and dealt with. With depression, one's whole life force seems collapsed. There is a lack of will to do anything. Sufferers can feel hopeless, as if there is no possibility and they cannot effect a change in their situation. It has recently been estimated that depression is one of the single biggest items in the UK National Health Service budget. It occurs at all ages and for all sorts of reasons.

This book is not about more complex psychological states and how to deal with them, this being left for more appropriate solutions already well-covered elsewhere, as in therapy or counselling. However for those on a journey who might feel depressed, as with other areas already covered, this is about self-enquiry, going within and asking what might be at the bottom of those depressed feelings, surfacing them, acknowledging them and dealing with what is going on that is leading to the depressed state. This can lead you to explore the repeat thoughts and belief patterns that we are covering in this Part.

Love

At the core of our being is love. This is who we really are. Yet, through the disappointments of life, we have learned to distance ourselves from it, even to distrust it or feel embarrassed around it. Psychologists say that the experience of separation from our mother and the upsets of childhood lead us to doubt love. When we find a loved one as a partner, we experience romantic love, directed towards another. Romantic love is often dulled and can even be replaced after a while by other feelings if the relationship does not go well. Love may still exist underneath, but the pain of the difficulty can obscure it. If or when we lose that person, we may feel a loss which may still seem like love but may not be. Sometimes loving someone is actually the experience of needing someone, again quite different. So we may confuse love with other experiences.

Love is simply that, a feeling of love. When we get in touch with our core beingness, we just feel love, pure and simple, love for ourselves, love for others and love of everything and of life itself. We are reminded of this love in all sorts of different encounters with life. It is a feeling that probably many of us connect with more frequently than we might imagine. We might notice it for example when in contact with small children, or in nature when affected by beautiful scenery, or when enjoying the company of friends, when we feel our hearts being touched.

Other feelings are often associated with love, such as joy, enthusiasm, warmth, bliss, pleasure, cheerfulness, playfulness, a sense of beauty, contentment. Within the Hindu tradition there are those who describe love as the "secret sensation of the Self", where I and the divine are regarded as One.

Love versus fear

The disruptive emotions described above can come and go. It is when we hold on to them that they cause us difficulty. Since the bottom-line disruptive emotion is fear, when we let that go, we are open to experiencing more love in our lives. The real work to do then is through self-awareness to become aware of those feelings, especially fear, and find ways to move through them. This allows a more centred state and also makes space for more love in our lives.

Letting go of disruptive feelings

Training ourselves to recognise and let go of disruptive feelings, therefore, is a key skill in growth, as we saw earlier.

- **Awareness**: Through self-awareness, we become aware that a disruptive feeling has us by the throat, so to speak.
- **Responsibility**: The key is then to take responsibility and to manage our state such that we can deal with the feeling and let it go.
- **Exploring it**: It could be that we need to go further into the feeling to find out what it is about, as was described with focusing in Part One. It could also be that there is some underlying concern that you need to surface and deal with.
- **Focus on the feeling**: However, if you wish to simply let the feeling go, one way to do this is to focus purely on the feeling. This often means letting go of any thought that fuels the feeling (see below). This is where the will plays a part. You need to keep the focus on the feeling and not go back to the thoughts. Keeping your awareness with the feeling, the art is to allow the feeling to be there just as a feeling. Simply hold it in your awareness and **feel** it. Keep feeling it, and also breathe into it....and it just dissolves of its own accord. This is the true letting go: **allowing** it to go, giving it up, not using an effort or forcing or suppressing.

This is what feelings naturally do. They come and go, passing through the body.

Is this who you really are?

Activity: Feelings you hang on to

What feelings do you hang on to? These would probably be ones you are attached to and which may now be no longer useful.

....
....
....
....
....
....
....

Perfectly simple. It's just that we are afraid of our disruptive feelings. And, as the saying goes, "what you resist persists". Resisting the feeling keeps it there.

Thoughts and feelings

Feelings are related to thoughts. The thought may give rise to a feeling. It might be an inbuilt pattern, such that you've built up an association between something happening, a thought you had about it and a feeling associated with the thought. You are no longer aware of the thought but when the circumstance occurs you get the feeling straight away. For example, when you hear a certain piece of music, you might immediately have a feeling association with something that once occurred around the time you were hearing that music. What can be useful is to identify the thought that is at the root of the repetitive feeling.

Patterns of thoughts

Here are some examples, in this case related to anxiety.

A child may not like going to school, perhaps because he finds aspects of being at school difficult or meets people on the way whom he is afraid of. So when it gets near to going to school he feels fearful and gets a pit in the stomach, with a sort of sickness and/or diarrhoea. It is actually a dread. As he grows up, he becomes able to deal with going to school, then college and finally work, but he continues to feel the sensations to some extent whenever he thinks about work. Knowing what is at the root of this pattern, his childhood fear of going to school helps him confront his fears. He knows the thoughts that link with the feelings.

A severe example of a repeat pattern is panic attacks. Panic attacks are physiological experiences that result in a pounding heart and acute shortness of breath. The actual physical cause is not clear, although the sufferer may be already predisposed to some form of anxiety. These attacks can be successfully managed, often with professional help. However, they can be very frightening if not understood and managed. The experiencer can make an inaccurate association in her mind between the attack and where she was when it first happened. Thus she starts to develop a phobia of that place, feeling terrified of the place and unable to go there. For example, if a panic attack happens in a supermarket, supermarkets become feared rather the underlying cause which was probably something that had happened some hours, days, weeks or even months before. It is an underlying anxiety that suddenly activates but the place in which it activates becomes the focus and believed cause. Repetitive thoughts then keep the fears in place.

Compulsive

It is important to remember that deeply embedded patterns like these take some unpicking. They become compulsive. We don't see them; they are outside our awareness. They are habits. We sometimes refer to them as "knee-jerk responses". Taking responsibility here means taking the time to spot when a compulsive thought/feeling pattern is at work.

Activity: Repetitive thoughts

Think of thoughts you keep regularly thinking. What thoughts do you often get wrapped up in? As you go about your day, notice each one and write it down:
....
....
....
....
....
....
....
....
....
....
....

They can be thoughts you have when you are caught up in some upset or are depressed. They could be ones that keep coming up when you are busy on your own and your mind is active thinking about things.

Thoughts and feelings

***Activity: Repetitive thoughts*:**

Now look at your list of repetitive thoughts. Which ones are helpful to you, which serve you?

....
....
....
....
....

Which ones evoke strong feelings in you?

....
....
....
....
....

Which ones really aren't useful, and maybe keep popping up and take you where you don't want to go?

....
....
....
....
....

The important thing here is to work to identify the really unhelpful thought/feeling patterns, so that they become less disruptive in your life.

Is this who you really are?

The guilt cycle

A good example of where thoughts and feelings work off each other is to be found in the more complex set of feelings called guilt. Here, the role of thoughts is all-pervasive.

Where we need to have some way of moderating our behaviour to enable us to live with others, guilt may be said to be useful, in the sense that it alerts us to something that we needed to do that might be missing. However, for everyday living it is often very unnecessary, since it is based on thoughts we have made up that we do not need.

Right/wrong

At a simple level, many of us grew up and learned to live with concepts of right and wrong. At one level this is very useful since we needed to learn and internalise ways of behaving that ensured we kept to commonly used beliefs and moral principles, like respect for other people, or adhering to the laws of the land. However, such thinking can get beyond what we need when we start to judge ourselves and others harshly or where it is not so necessary.

A classic example is where a person constantly tells herself that she is at fault, that what she is doing is in some way wrong. What particularly pushes her buttons is when another person may question what she is doing or why she has or has not done something. She immediately thinks she has done something wrong and then gets very defensive. All the other person was doing was to try to find something out and did not have a judgement about it. As a child she was often in trouble for, as she saw it, "doing things wrong". So she feels thoroughly guilty.

What has happened is that we take on board societal rules, the "social consensus", and make them our own without really deciding whether they are truly useful.

The guilt cycle

Maybe now is the time to decide which "rules" really do serve us and give up judging ourselves or others when we don't need to. And we can make the rules we keep to be our rules, ones we own.

Judgements

Seeing things in right/wrong terms is an example of judging. Other examples are: good/bad; better/worse; superior/inferior; winner/loser. We judge ourselves and others. We compare one person against another and ourselves with other people. The standards we are using are ours. Although we may think they are commonly held, they may well be based on our own perceptions or on the "social consensus" that we have taken on board without questioning.

Blame

When someone has broken the law and caused another harm, they are blamed by the law-enforcement authorities. But we use the idea of blame in a more mundane and less useful way, the Blame Game.

The Blame Game is widespread. Part of victim thinking is blame: where we don't take responsibility. According to this pattern, what occurs in my life that I don't like is due to other people. Language which reveals this is, "you make me feel…" or "someone made me do this" or "because things were like this, I had to…" Somehow, others seem to be calling the shots. It is rife in certain organisations, and is referred to as a "blame culture".

Guilt

Once found wanting, you are judged guilty. Used as part of your own inner dialogue this is destructive. It also gives power to others who will tap into your guilty feelings and accuse you such that inadvertently you dance to their tune.

Failure

One form of guilt is where we have failed to live up to our own inner standards, and we thus judge ourselves a failure. Fear of failure is a common trait among people at work. Those for example who are very career-motivated may give themselves a very hard time if they are not successful in their careers. Or if something goes wrong in their work, they may judge themselves or others harshly because they see it as a failure.

Punishment

As we get towards the end of the cycle, judgement is passed and we must now receive our punishment. We punish ourselves and others for transgressions. For example, when we do something that we feel is wrong, we hit a table with our fist or bash the wall in anger or hit our heads with our hands. We blame ourselves and now we must be punished. While this seems very harmless, it isn't really because we are hurting ourselves, beating ourselves up. It is highly likely that we will do the same to others.

Shame

At the end of the cycle, with punishment comes shame. In medieval times in England, people were punished in a very shaming way by being placed in wooden stocks in the street where people could see them, laugh or scold them and throw things like rotten food at them. More recently small children at school would be "shamed" for a transgression by being told to stand in a corner with their face to the corner. They would be shamed in public. One might say that that still carries on today when we publicly find fault with one another. The media speaks of people being "publicly shamed" for their deeds.

People feel shame very deeply, more powerfully than guilt. Shame is where we get to feel very bad about ourselves and our unworthiness, where we feel deeply at fault. Feelings of shame are so strong that they can be described as a sense of rottenness at our core. Embarrassment is a common way it is experienced, where the person

The guilt cycle

will go very red in the face. They want to hide their face and their body and not be seen.

At the root of a lot of guilt is low self-esteem, not loving and valuing ourselves. What we need to do is to reverse that, to start respecting and loving ourselves. Then when guilt comes up you can start telling yourself that you do not need this feeling, and work to give it up.

Activity: Reflecting on your guilt

In what ways do you feel some aspect of guilt? Make a note here:
....
....
....
....
....
....
....

Then ask yourself: Is this really serving you? Is it really useful?
....
....
....

If the feeling of guilt involves the attitude or behaviour of another who seems aggrieved, you might also need to have closure with the person concerned.

Is this who you really are?

Resentment

Resentment is anger against someone which we hold on to and don't resolve. Firstly we are still feeling it and it is very probably not doing us any good. Unreleased anger eats away in our body and we can get ill as a result. I once heard it described as drinking poison while wishing ill of another. Secondly, it often poisons our relationships in some way.

Holding on to past wrongs

So, it might be worth asking yourself what you are holding on to from the past. What transgressions are you feeling angry about, or bitter about, or simply wish it had been different in some way:

Activity: People who have transgressed

Make a list of these transgressions: Think of your family, friends you have or had, partners you are with or are no longer with, fellow school pupils, work colleagues, previous jobs, past or present bosses, neighbours, etc.. Who in particular did you wrong and you've not forgotten it. When their name comes to mind, check within yourself: how do you feel?

....
....
....
....
....
....
....
....
....
....

This is serious life laundry. We really need to look at those people and incidents and wrongs that we still hold on to. Be honest with yourself. Sometimes we don't like to admit that we still harbour a grudge.

Resentment

You might also think of incidents that keep recurring, where you end up feeling a lot about what someone did and not letting go of it. Where has this come from?

How it eats away: bitterness

Resentment at its worst is bitterness. What that does to your body is self-corrosive. For example, it is said that one condition associated with bitterness is arthritis. Another is to the face: a person will in time appear as if they are all "eaten up", as the face holds the feeling in its musculature. What we are talking about here is a subtle form of continuing rage. It is likely to be in the atmosphere around the person and impact their on-going contact with others.

When it is body-related, as above, it is a form of **retroflection**, where energy is directed into the body rather than outwards as anger might more normally operate. Energy retroflected unhealthily eats away at the body. We suffer.

A good book to read on what our mind does to our body is *You can heal your life* by Louise Hay[14]. See especially her chart of various body ailments and their mind connections. Another very useful book is *The Healing Power of Illness* by Thorwald Dethlefsen and Rudiger Dahlke[15].

Letting go

To let go of this often means several things. Firstly we need to take responsibility for what we are feeling. Then we can take action to get it out of our system. Here are two steps one can take:

---

[14] Louise Hay, *You can heal your life*, Carlsbad, CA, Hay House, 1984
[15] Thorwald Dethlefsen and Rudiger Dahlke, *The Healing Power of Illness*, English edition: Shaftesbury, UK, 1990 and Rockport MA, USA, Element Books,, 1991

Is this who you really are?

i. Express how you feel safely

It can help to find a place away from other people where you can sound off, and then to really get into it, maybe shouting out how you feel, hitting cushions, or using some hard object like a baseball bat on an old foam mattress. Find a way in which you can safely work out your anger without cost to yourself or others. Sitting in a stationary car with the engine running can be good too (but don't go driving it till you've cooled off!)

You could write the person a letter, which you don't post but instead burn. If you had a photo, you could take it out on the photo. Really tell them how you feel.

You might go and see the person. However, while that is often a good way of getting things out into the open, you will need to be assertive and non-blaming, working from ownership; otherwise you might fuel the fire.

Most resentment is something we need to let go of in ourselves.

There are now a lot of programmes on anger management available.

ii. Forgive

In letting go of resentment, we are giving something up. This is forgiveness. We don't, in a sense, go up to someone and say, "I forgive you", meaning "I'll let you off this time", implying that he or she is the lucky one or that you'll be watching her or him in future! Forgiveness is something that happens **inside you**: you truly **give something up**. You truly and honestly let go of resentment and give up the right to punish.

You might take a picture, or visualise the person, and in your mind's eye bring to mind how you have felt. You might use the focusing technique described in the first part of this book. Then, take some deeper breaths and breathe out those feelings, say "I forgive you" and then allow yourself to let it go. Maybe tell yourself that you are letting

Resentment

it go. Then, in the future, whenever those thoughts come up again, say "I'm letting .....go". Really challenge those thoughts each time they recur.

For a good book on forgiveness see *Radical Forgiveness* by Colin C. Tipping[16].

Activity: Giving up resentment

What resentments would you be willing to give up and how?

....
....
....
....
....
....
....
....
....
....

---

[16] Colin C. Tipping, *Radical Forgiveness,* USA, Global 13 Publications, 1998

Is this who you really are?

Anxiety and worry

As seen earlier, anxiety is essentially fear-based. We worry about what might happen. "What if…" So it is future-related. "It" hasn't happened yet. Of course it might not happen. But the worrier is afraid it might. She lacks faith and trust. She might catastrophise: if this happened then what else might happen? So the feared outcome gets magnified.

The worry habit

Worry can become a form of habit. Then it is repetitive. For example, I might start to look for things to worry about. If I'm not worrying, then I might be missing something. I scan my mental horizon for something I ought to be thinking about, to take care about, and in other words worry about. I wake up worrying, not only in the morning but potentially in the middle of the night.

Another example might be when a man does not come home when expected. The partner starts to worry. Maybe he's just delayed at the office. Maybe he's having trouble with his manager yet again. As time goes by, she is surprised that he hasn't called. She calls but gets his voice-mail. Maybe he's delayed on the way. Maybe he's having an affair. Maybe he's had an accident. And so it goes on. The woman creates a whole story of her partner's adventures, probably very unrelated to what has actually happened, which is that his train was stuck in an area where there was no signal and he couldn't call her.

What it does to your body

Worry also eats at the system. It is often associated with the stomach ("butterflies in the stomach"), intestines and bowel. Worriers can feel like they need the bathroom. This is the flight part of the flight/fight response kicking into action, except that it gets repetitive. The heart is affected, since fear causes the heart to beat faster. There may also be tension in the body ("gripped by fear"). A worrier tends to have a serious look ("a knitted brow") and become "lined with worry".

Anxiety and worry

Activity: What do you worry about and what does it do to you?

....
....
....
....
....
....
....

Manifesting what you fear

It is worth thinking about what we might be setting ourselves up for by worry. People often say, "My worst fear came true...." It did actually happen. As we saw earlier, thought is creative. What we think, we become. Keep thinking a certain outcome and you are more likely to make it happen, at some level.

Like guilt, it is a useless way of thinking. It hasn't happened. And surely it is more effective to focus positively on desired outcomes? So, how might you give it up?

Using present-moment awareness

Bring your awareness into the present moment. Breathe deeply. Breathe in strongly. Visualise yourself drawing breath down into the stomach area, into your power centre, drawing down power into the area when action is generated energetically, and as you breathe out imagine in your mind's eye breathing out fear and anxiety, letting it go. Focus on the present moment. That is all that exists. Let your body relax.

Bring your will into play. Deliberately choose to let go of the thoughts around the worry. Stop those thoughts. Use your breath if necessary, breathing away the thoughts. If the worry is strong, shift your awareness to the feeling instead. Feel the feeling and allow the energy of fear to pass through you and out. This technique was described in the part on "Feelings" earlier.

Is this who you really are?

Another approach is to let go of the desired outcome. Sometimes worry is generated because in worrying about an unwanted outcome we are allowing ourselves to be too attached to the original outcome. We've made it too important. Is it really so crucial to your survival? So, try letting it go. Surrender to the present moment. Give it up to the universe, to God, to Life or whatever.

A great book to read on managing fear in personal growth is *Feel the fear and do it anyway* by Susan Jeffers[17]

---

[17] Susan Jeffers, *Feel the fear and do it anyway*, Harcourt, USA, 1987

Desire and need

In Yogic philosophy desire is a root thought behind a lot of our thinking. We want and we want and we want. What we have is not enough.

We've generated a whole economic system around unmet desire: when I've got that car, that house, that job, that wife/husband/partner, etc., then I'll be OK. Hence we work like mad to get the money or the partner we want. However, when we get there, it's perhaps good for a bit and then we look around for something else.

We also fear we have something to lose and so hold on like mad to what we've got. Thus we get powerfully invested in defence of our possessions, our partner, our money, our lifestyle, or other things that we give value to. It can seem to some that if they lose these things, they'll be staring into the abyss.

At the root of unmet desire is our experience of separation from the whole. We know that because we always have a sense that something is missing.

An associated root thought is that we have need, since we think that to survive we must get our needs met. There must be something outside of us that we need in order to be happy. At one level that might seem very obvious. At another, a more trusting level, our needs always get met, so in a sense we have no needs. One who sees that she is her own source of happiness, has no needs.

However, we believe we have needs and on that root thought, a whole lot more thoughts are developed.

Expectations

One development of need is that we have expectations from life and other people. We want others to behave in a particular way, as we think they should. For me to feel OK, others have to show up.

Is this who you really are?

Firstly this puts a lot of pressure on others, which they might resist, or it puts a lot of pressure on you. Secondly, it is an abdication of personal responsibility. Somehow, it leaves us dependent on other people and potentially liable to push out a whole load of resentment on to them if they don't fulfil our expectations. Also it is a set-up for disappointment and unmet desire. And so the cycle will go on.

Basically, catch yourself creating an expectation and give it up. Instead, ask yourself what you could be intending for yourself here. You will need to do it unconditionally, having really let it go. You might then find – magic! – that they do what you had wanted, but with a whole lot more freedom.

Jealousy

It is quite simple. The other person has something you want. You haven't got it, but they have. So you feel anger towards them. Jealousy is another way of being that eats away inside. It is a quiet fury. Envy is its partner. It can be very nasty, because it usually involves some nastiness directed at another. People usually find jealousy very unattractive, probably because they fear you might direct it towards them instead. They feel unsafe and pull away. Otherwise, you might just sit there and feel jealous.

It is quite simply an utterly unrewarding approach to life, which leaves us miserable. So, as with so many of the thought-based activities of the mind that we are exploring, we need to find some way to take responsibility and to give it up as useless.

It is also useful to look at what is generating the thoughts and feelings as well. A jealous person is, as we have seen with desire, operating out of need, the sense that something is missing. What they really need to do is deal with the hole inside them which the sense of need is expressing.

"There's not enough"

Somehow with desire, there is a belief that there is not enough around. An obvious way this is perceived is that there is not enough food, not enough resources, and so on. Another is where people feel they do not have enough money, a very common experience. Whatever happens, somehow there is not enough there.

- **"Not enough love"** is one form. Many a person is searching for love outside, because he feels a hole inside him and believes he can fill it by finding someone else who will love him. What he is experiencing is a "need for love". However he confuses it with "love", which is quite different. So when he is in relationship, his relating is fuelled by a **deficit need**, wanting love from another. This gets compounded when he also feels that he does not "get enough" from his partner, that the partner does "not do enough" for him, is "not there enough" for him, and so on. Another way this is experienced is that he is "needy": he is aware that he feels so uncomfortable inside himself that he needs another person to somehow make it "all right". Obviously one can see the emotional dependency on another that this can create.

- **"I am not enough"**: A person might also turn the experience of "not enough" on themselves. They might believe they are "not good enough". Whatever they do, which might be mountains for another, somehow the experience is they don't do enough, don't perform well enough, are not "up to the mark", and so on. What is fuelling this is that inside they have low self esteem but think they need others' approval in order to feel OK.

- **Satisfaction/dissatisfaction cycles** can flow from the same sense of deficit need. A person may think she can't be satisfied and as a result is always searching for something outside her to satisfy her. People who run businesses can be like that, showing a restless searching for something more, better, bigger, something more successful. The career drive to be successful can be fuelled by feeling inadequate in this way: if I succeed I

Is this who you really are?

can prove to others or to myself that I'm good enough. The trouble for the successful business person is that, having really made it, they one day wake up and ask themselves, "There's got to be more than this". The restless search for satisfaction could just go on – or they instead start to ask themselves what all this is really about, and start to work on themselves.

Otherwise what we think, we get: "I want" creates a want, a lack. "Wanting" does not fundamentally get a result.

Activity: Your desires and needs

What are your desires and needs, the ones that keep coming up?
....
....
....
....
....
....

Focus on the feeling

What we need to do is to take the real desire, the wanting for something to fill the hole inside us, which we've pushed out there to get our needs met, and focus on it, really feel it. This can be scary because it brings us into contact with our existential fear described earlier, that perhaps we are nothing, or when we die we may be nothing, abandoned, alone. The sense of need is a hole, something missing. Remember that to deal with fear, we can allow ourselves to feel the feeling and let it dissolve because it is an illusion like the rest.

Lynne Twist, who works as a charity fundraiser, stresses in *The Soul of Money*[18] that "Sufficiency isn't an amount at all". She says that it is a belief, a statement, an experience, and a context that we create that there is enough.

---

[18] Lynne Twist, *The Soul of Money*, New York, Norton, 2003, p. 74.

Desire and need

Thus there is a further step. As you focus on yourself in this way, allow yourself to have the understanding that inside you somewhere there is another self, your real Self. This Self is whole and is full to the brim and beyond with love. It is joy. It is contentment. It is always satisfied. It is laughter. It is lightness. It is going to have a ball. When we contact our real selves, there is no sense of being inadequate, "not enough", nothing or having nothing when instead we are full to the brim with joy and upliftment. Learn instead to allow yourself to contact this part of you that really values, loves and respects yourself for who you are.

Use an affirmation like "I love and respect myself just as I am", and repeat it to yourself regularly. Start to love yourself. As the song goes, "It is the greatest love of all".

Is this who you really are?

Beliefs

As we saw earlier, beliefs have a powerful effect. What we believe manifests in our lives. The world reflects back to us our own beliefs: what seems to go on "out there" mirrors what is going on inside. Beliefs are very core to us. They can be dear to us or at least the ones we hold on to, very often outside our awareness.

Beliefs are based on decisions you've made, about life, other people, and yourself.

Activity: Your beliefs about yourself

What beliefs do you have about yourself? Go and look at yourself in a mirror. Take a very good look, up close, and then at a distance. Do you like what you see? What are your opinions about you? Write them down:
....
....
....
....
....
....

What beliefs do you have about your life, other people, and life in general? Without thinking too much, complete these sentences:

Life is..

People are..

My life is..

It can be useful to identify any core underlying beliefs that do not serve you, such as "People are not to be trusted". "People let me down". "I am unattractive". How honest have you been? Check through your replies. It is what's truthful that matters. When we know what disempowering and de-motivating messages we've been giving ourselves, we can set about changing them.

Studying yourself in a mirror can be useful later too. As you get to like yourself more you can start to appreciate yourself in a mirror and look deeply into your own inner beauty in your own eyes. They say that "the eyes are the windows of the soul".

Beliefs about yourself

As we have seen, it is the negative beliefs we hold about ourselves that are the most disempowering. And yet these sorts of beliefs are widespread in humanity. Welcome to the human race. Very many of us underneath hold beliefs about ourselves like these: I am unworthy; I'm not good enough; I am a bad person; I am unlikeable; I am useless; I am ugly; I am fat; nobody likes me; nobody is there for me; I am unlovable; I dislike myself; I hate myself.

This reads as some horrible list, but so many of us think that inside, or at least when we're feeling particularly unhappy. We may also think that others think that of us. We can find that in the world too: unworthiness, untrustworthiness, badness, ugliness, lack of love, hate. This is what we can create. The world mirrors back to us what we feel inside.

An example might be someone who is bullied at work. People are much more aware of this in today's workplace and there is now support in place in many environments to help. However, for the one who experiences bullying, it is a horrible experience, leaving one feeling very alone, demoralised and with low self-esteem. Let us say that one person, Andy (not his real name), is a strong-minded individual who tends to think he is right in situations and likes to have his own way. He also likes a joke, especially if it is at another's expense. Another whom he works with, whom we'll call Damian likes to collaborate with people and is generally supportive and helpful. He is sensitive however to criticism and tends to take things a bit personally. As they work together, Andy tends to pick holes in what Damian is doing and points out where things are not working, usually

Is this who you really are?

at Damian's expense. In social situations, Andy also makes subtle jokes that are aimed at Damian and that others find funny. Damian at first stands his ground about the criticism, but when Andy responds aggressively, he backs off and simply responds defensively by pointing out what he thinks he has done right. He now doesn't push back when this treatment occurs, and when the "humour" is being used he simply laughs weakly. His work suffers and he finds his manager is becoming concerned about his performance. She decides to discuss it with him, observe what is going on and ask others, and fortunately for Damian realises what is happening.

One might say that Damian simply needs to learn to be more assertive and stand his ground, were it not that deeper forces are at work which underline how this isn't easy for him. In Damian's case, as a child he was the subject of parental physical abuse by his father, who would hit him repeatedly. His mother never came to his aid and he was unable to do anything about his situation. All he would do is try to be "nice" and cheerful, to try to please his father and thus hope that his father wouldn't be angry with him. Yet his boundaries would be repeatedly violated, whenever his father was stressed or had been drinking. As children do he blamed himself, thinking that he must be so unworthy and at fault that his father would be so displeased with him. His low self-esteem meant that it was hard for him to stand up for himself at school and he was frequently bullied. All he could do is try and be nice to people and hope it would go away. However, the treatment followed him around. People who are bullied more easily attract bullies to them. Others would somehow sense he did not value himself and therefore certain less well-disposed people did not respect him and would dish out further punishment.

This situation is all too common. The root issue is low self-esteem, not loving and valuing oneself. If we respect ourselves, others will too. In Damian's case, the pleaser tactic didn't work, because people sensed an inauthenticity behind it, in that what he really wanted was for people to like him. But why should they when he so plainly did not like himself. There was a whole lot of work for him to do to heal his childhood wound, to help himself to get in touch with his own power, to make clear boundaries with people about what was OK and what was not, to assert himself, and also crucially to value and respect himself.

Self-esteem: loving and valuing yourself

The truth you can discover is that those negative beliefs, being bad, useless, unlikeable or whatever, however painful are not who you are. They are what you've made up about yourself. They are powerful and we really do hang on to them. But to move on, we need to let them go and adopt other more positive beliefs. After all, we are making all this up. Why hang on to beliefs that keep us stuck and are not who we really are? So why not go for something more empowering?

There's a famous passage by Marianne Williamson[19]: "Our deepest fear is that we are powerful beyond measure." We fear and doubt our greatness, when we are actually all meant to shine. As children of God, she asks, who are we to hide our light? Our playing small does not serve the world. It certainly does not serve us.

To start loving ourselves is a conscious decision, a choice, an act of will. We use the mind in our true service. How can you do this? For some this does not take a lot, for others it is a long road and they will also need support elsewhere. There are now many organisations and individuals working to help people boost their self-esteem.

Here are some fairly simple steps that people have taken. For some they seem challenging, and that is part of the process, shifting into a mode of **Valuing You**.

Self-esteem actions

This is by no means a complete list. I would encourage you to come up with some of your own too:

---

[19] Marianne Williamson, *A Return to Love*, UK revised edition, London, Thorsons, 1996, p. 190.

Is this who you really are?

i. Make the decision to love yourself: commit to it

"**I love and appreciate myself**". Even if you don't feel like it, the point is to make the decision. Thought is creative. You've put it out there, and you will now start the process of drawing to you what you need to support you in the process.

There will be times when you think, "but I don't love myself"; "That's crazy"; "I'm ugly"; "I'm being selfish"; etc, etc. The ego jumps up and questions it. The point is to stick with your intention. What you may be experiencing is resistance. Challenge these thoughts. They are not who you are.

ii. A self-appreciation exercise

Give yourself some time to care for yourself.

Maybe take a long, hot, luxurious bath, with lots of bubbles. Really take your time to wash yourself. As you wash each part of your body, tell that part how special and valuable it is. Thank it for the part it plays in your life. If you come to parts you don't like, acknowledge it in some way for being there to teach you something. In reality this is a negative perception about that part, which you are holding on to and which you need to let go of.

Another way to do this is to lie down, take a deeper breath to relax yourself, and then to run your mind's eye over your body slowly, giving attention to each part in turn. Then you find something positive to say about each part as above.

iii. An affirmation

Design an affirmation for yourself. Affirmations are positive statements about something you intend or wish to create. They are stated in the present tense as if they are happening now, and the idea is that you repeat them to yourself over time. What you are doing is using the creative power of thought to work for you.

Beliefs

Activity: Appreciating yourself

Choose an affirmation:
"I love, value and respect myself"
"I am a good and special person"
"I am beautiful, just as I am"
"I honour myself for who I am"
"I am love, bliss and joy without end"

Write down one that you like:

....
....
....

Use it daily, for example in the last two minutes of a meditation, repeating it over to yourself plenty of times. Say it too at other times of the day. Keep doing this for at least 30 days. You might find after a while that you will feel tempted to stop it, especially if it seems not to be working. This is crucial because your resistance to what you are doing is coming out. That is exactly when you will need to redouble the effort to keep on track. I will say more about staying on track in the last part of the book.

To read more about affirmations, see *You can Heal Your Life* by Louise Hay referred to earlier. See also *Creative Visualisation* by Shakti Gawain[20].

iv. Review your routine

Take a good look at how you live your life daily. How much time do you give to yourself, as opposed to others or to your work? Write down the routine, noting how long you spend on each activity.

Arrange some "you" time, when you can do more of what you need for you. How about a time to meditate or pray; a time for reflection; time to read an inspiring book; to draw; to write? Do you need to find some activity for yourself that would nurture yourself regularly? What

---

[20] Shakti Gawain, *Creative Visualisation*, Bantam, New York, 1982

Is this who you really are?

about regular exercise for your body? Most of us don't get enough exercise for our long-term health. What about time with friends, or with the family or with your loved one if you have a partner.

    v.   **Your health, food and life style**

Nourishing our body is a key part of the process. Low self-esteem is expressed in the body in some form, often in weight levels or poor eating patterns. So, take a review of how healthy your diet is, what your fitness level is, and whether your life-style is really serving you. Look at your alcohol consumption, smoking, and any other potentially addictive substances. Such substance intake, and over-eating, is a way of disconnecting from painful feelings and therefore not taking responsibility for them.

    vi.   **Clean up and do up your house**

Does your house or apartment need a life-laundry? Do you have rooms full of stuff you don't use? When was it last properly cleaned? Does it need re-decorating? Could you spruce it up to reflect the new you?

    vii.   **Look at your clothes**

Could you change your image for something more self-valuing? People often express themselves in their dress. This may be the time for a refit. Get some feedback from your friends. See an image consultant.

    viii.   **Special times for you: treats**

Give yourself a good time regularly. Take yourself somewhere where you'd really like to go. This is about giving to yourself.

    ix.   **Support available**

Get a coach. Coaching is a great way to set empowering goals, address what gets in the way, explore choices and ways forward and motivate yourself to take action towards achieving what you really want. There are also bodies that can help with self-esteem. See an international body that fosters self-esteem, with resources and information: www.self-esteem-international.org. Also see the National Association for Self-Esteem, a US organisation that supports building self-esteem. Their book list indicates the wealth of material on the subject.

Valuing/loving others

When we start to love ourselves, this process naturally extends to others. People sometimes fear that self-esteem work is "selfish", as if they "shouldn't" do it but "must" put others first. One can almost hear the inner critic at work, applying rules that originate from other people. We have a right to value ourselves. Then we can truly love others unconditionally, without a deficit need. A full heart overflows into the world at large. We start to smile naturally to others, without expecting one in return. A person full of love becomes naturally and spontaneously generous and kind-hearted. They naturally extend courtesies and kindnesses to others, not out of some rule or principle that they've internalised from others but because it seems totally natural, as part of being a loving being.

The key is to smile authentically, unconditionally, without any expectation of anything in return. This is an act of generosity, of love towards your fellow humans. It is something to practice. People tend to reciprocate unconditional smiles in some way. It is infectious, like laughter. So what you get back is the warmth of humanity.

I've been doing this for some time now. It just happens naturally. I started doing it in shops and when I made way for others in crowded areas. I found that a pure, simple natural smile got a response every now and again. Now I do it all over the place.

Try it! Go out and start extending your love to others, unconditionally. A smile costs nothing. See how good you feel!

Is this who you really are?

Separation

At the root of human unhappiness, some argue, lies the experience of separateness. This is the sense of being alone, apart, different, isolated. It has links with feeling unloved, which has been referred to in the section on "Beliefs". Writers in the 20th Century made much of the despair of the human condition, as seen in the writings of some of the Existentialists. They argued that a "given" of being human is to be alone and we leave this life alone.

Although this has already been referred to in other parts of this book, it is being mentioned again here partly because the experience of isolation, of being unloved, and the attendant fears about death, is so profound as to potentially contradict what is being discussed. It is important, therefore to point out this experience in order to help people through it.

A very useful book for those who are interested in deeper inner work is *Soul Power* by Nikki de Carteret[21]. She has an excellent section on the "Dark Night of the Soul". The Dark Night is where we get confronted with our underlying barriers to growth, where we may face a real crisis of faith, in who we are, in what we believe, in our potential for healing and in our ultimate happiness. Nikki says that each dark night comes to show you what needs to shift within you.

When we encounter the existential experiences referred to here, it is important to face them and work them through, for they are truly a gift, which is the opposite of what many might think. These experiences lie at the root of many people's issues. We spend a huge amount of energy trying to avoid them.

As with other dilemmas discussed already, we need to face, embrace and feel what we fear, feel the fear, and allow the fear to dissolve, to let it go. It is quite simply an illusion. We also need to build up our awareness of who we really are, which will be discussed in the next two sections, and learn to love ourselves and know our core essence of

---

[21] Nikki de Carteret, *Soul Power*, Alresford, Hampshire, UK, O Books, 2003

Separation

joy, bliss, love, contentment, fun and laughter and the other qualities of who we are. And we need to let go of our attachment to those maladaptive thoughts, feelings and behaviours that form part of the Ego. The Dark Night is a confrontation with our core stuff. It is an illusion which in Sanskrit, an ancient Indian classical language, is called *maya*.

To feel separate is to feel "apart" from the whole, from life, the universe, nature, beauty, God, Allah, or whichever term you prefer, which is what we ultimately long to be "a part" of, and which we can come to find we are "a part" of. Our journey, arguably, is to know that place.

An excellent book that describes the experience of oneness and is full of ideas to support you on your path to know that place is Marianne Williamson's book, *A Return to Love*[22]. Another one is *Boundless Love* by Miranda Holden[23]. You can read more about the phenomenon of the Dark Night of the Soul in the book by Thomas More[24].

---

[22] Marianne Williamson, *A Return to Love*, New York, HarperCollins, 1992
[23] Miranda Holden, *Boundless Love,* London, Rider, 2002
[24] Thomas More, *Dark Nights of the Soul*, New York, Penguin USA, 2004.

Is this who you really are?

Letting go again

Often to connect with who we really are, we need to let go. That is sometimes something that happens effortlessly. Sometimes we need to work on it. Sometimes it requires a conscious effort of will.

As was said earlier, you need **awareness**, and then you need to take **responsibility** for what is occurring in you, exercise **choice** and then **let it go**. You may simply drop it and in fact you can learn to do this as a matter of course. With greater practice you will gain more mastery and then you can do that.

At other times, you may need to work through what is coming up for you such that you can accept it for what it is, knowing it is not part of you at essence. You may need to deal with how it came to be there in the first place and what has kept it in place. Then you can school yourself to start to let it go. This might mean every time that thought, feeling or behaviour comes up, you notice it and choose not to get into it. However if it's really got you, you may have to work through it and start to tell yourself to let it go. Eventually you will find it just goes. But, as I said, you will need to work on it. And remember the 80/20 principle: every now and again it might come back. But tell yourself that's just the 20% of your life. The 80% of your life is what you are growing into.

Letting go is something you find in your own way and learn to use in a way that means something to you. You may need help to really get this, which is why taking responsibility may also mean that reaching out for the help of others, including if necessary skilled professionals, may be just what you need to help you develop skill in doing it for yourself. Yet it is possible. What is happening is that you are training yourself to do it, parting the veils of illusion and discovering the truth and majesty of who you are.

And this brings us full circle, back to knowing who we really are. It might seem like an awful lot of pain, working on your ego. However it isn't always like that. There are also moments of great joy and insight and in fact many travellers along this way will report that they felt full

Letting go again

of inspiration, enthusiasm and commitment. For them there is no other way, because it is bringing them back to themselves.

People often report that many of the really big insights are very simple. Very often I've met people who have said that when they did some really powerful work on themselves, somehow at some point everything that they had been struggling with just dropped away and a whole new space opened up wherein all they were aware of was an all-encompassing love. Who they really were was right there in that moment. It was like coming home.

This sort of experience is described more fully in the next part of this book.

Part 3: Knowing your Inner Self

What dwells within us

Within us dwells a far more positive Self, one that many of us are usually only dimly aware of. Our focus in this book has been to examine ways in which we can move beyond our limited self so as to enjoy the fruits of this deeper Self. This part will build a picture of how that Self may be viewed, although in truth words are at times inadequate at this point and it is something that each of us must find his or her own way to experiencing and knowing – and making sense of according to her or his own frame of reference.

After all as we have seen, we are making all this up, each in our own way. The curious thing is though that when we each look deeply at it, it has a ring of truth that we each can acknowledge as if we all really share it.

So in this part we go deeper into the nature of the Self and start to explore what we might discover about who we really are as we free ourselves of the Ego's power over us. We will also look at some of the Ego's typical behaviours so that you can start to identify more clearly when your Ego is at work.

The Ego and the Real Self

We experience life within bounds. We seem to know it to be limited. Life seems to offer suffering, difficulty and struggle. Not that it always seems like that exactly, but often we encounter difficulties with others, with circumstances and with ourselves. Many talk, write, compose and think of unhappiness and unfulfillment, of unsatisfied desire, that something is missing. This experience of the limited personality we describe as that of the Ego.

The Ego as the limited self

Ego is a Latin word meaning "I". As it is used in this book, the term "ego" is understood not as Freud used it. It is here meant in the Eastern sense as the "I" of the small self, the personality that we've developed over time, the collection of sensing, feeling, thought and behaviour that does not serve us. It is a collection of past impressions, perceptions, understandings about who we are, who others are, ways of relating, and behaviours that we think define who we are. It consists of perceptions based on inaccurate interpretations. It is also equivalent to a term used in the East for this way of being. In Sanskrit it is called *ahamkara* and is also referred to as "the veil of suffering". It is the limited self. This veil conceals the real Self.

It has served us well in that it has looked after us, has enabled us to make creative adjustments to the circumstances and life events we have encountered, and has enabled us to survive. However, that is what it is, a survival mechanism that limits our potential.

The "small" self and the "great" Self

To continue with Eastern meanings, Sanskrit also uses the term *Atman* for the Self that is greater by far than the Ego, and is who we really are. The great Self is indescribable to the sages whose sayings were written in Sanskrit eons ago. They can however describe its qualities: the sages of Vedanta for example said that the Self was *Satchitananda*, *sat* meaning ever-existent or permanently real, *chit*

Knowing your inner self

meaning aware of itself and everything else, or conscious, and *ananda* meaning bliss or joy.

The great Self or Inner Self is who we really are. Some compare it with the natural or free self of the small child, spontaneous, fun-loving, authentic and honest, full of laughter, playful, fully in the moment. The great Self knows joy, unconditional love, contentment, enthusiasm, humour, spontaneity, aliveness. Those who have experienced this state in its fullness talk of waves of bliss, *ananda*.

Tony Parsons, in his wonderful little book *The Open Secret* describes his experience thus: As he was walking across a park,

> "A total stillness and presence seemed to descend over everything. All and everything became timeless and I no longer existed. I vanished and there was no longer an experiencer. Oneness with all and everything is what happened....and an overwhelming love filled every part. Together with this there came a total comprehension of the whole."[25]

We can have touches of these experiences, but generally they are short-lived. Those who embark in earnest on a self-development path often talk of experiences which take them briefly into this state, and they speak of it as life-changing. For example, they say that they felt full of love for weeks and months on end, although the experience reduces in time. What devotees do is take up practices that help them re-connect with this experience anew in a way that is increasingly unattached and over time reduces the effect of the Ego in dragging them back to the so-called "reality" of the limited, unfulfilled self.

The Ego is very pervasive. It is concerned with safety and survival. It keeps us separate. It is what we know; after all we've grown up with it and it seems to be very familiar and safe. It says, "Don't worry, I'll look after you." It might not be perfect, but in its imperfection, it seems to be the best we've got. It can even masquerade as a reformed person! It will repeatedly pop up, which is why persistence and

---

[25]Tony Parsons, *The Open Secret*, Dorset, UK, Open Secret Publishing, 1995, p.19.

The ego and the real self

commitment on the path of growth is so important. The thing to remember is that the great Self is also there, as we saw with the Witness, our "already always knowing". We just need to learn how to tap more into it.

The Self

In the other parts, reference has been made firstly to the self, the part of us whom we grew up as and which is heavily influenced by perception, and secondly the real Self which is who we really are. The distinction has been deliberately exaggerated for the purposes of this book. However, these are not two different characters within us, but rather facets of us. Through personal growth we learn to let go of those aspects that we have said are part of our Ego and that do not serve us or which we no longer wish to be part of our being. They don't necessarily vanish just like that but recede more into the background. The point is that we get less attached to them so that they less and less drive our lives. However, there is a far greater part of us that has been obscured but which is always present, our "already always knowing". With growth, this part is felt more and more and also we are able to live more and more in its light.

More on the small self and great Self

One way of viewing this distinction is to call these different facets the small self and the great Self. As we have seen, in Sanskrit the small self is called *ahamkara*, meaning ego, the individual "I", while the greater self is called *purnoham*, meaning the pure, universal "I". As we have been stressing, through practice and perseverance it is possible to increase your awareness of the latter.

The small self is identified with the contents of the mind, its thoughts, feelings and patterns. It also makes a connection between my identity and my body, viewing the body at some level as part of "me".

It is important to remember that the great Self is something that is experienced. Each will come to know it in his or her own way. Here are some ways that it might be experienced:

The Self

Some characteristics of the Great Self

- A feeling of joy in life right now, a sense of upliftment, maybe a thrill in living
- Feeing expansive and optimistic about life and the world
- Not being caught up in the Ego, in one's "mind stuff"
- Having a detachment; being aware of our body or our mind as something to be seen objectively
- Our minds are quiet or in the background
- A sense of connectedness, of being part of the whole, or at one with life, rather than feeling separate
- Feeling full of love, both for oneself and for everything and everyone around
- Taking spontaneous and appropriate action, without effort or pressure
- Timelessness
- Peace
- Attention is vividly present and this Present seems boundless
- Without assessing or judging or projecting, both ourselves and others
- Compassion towards others
- Contentment
- Trust
- Humour bubbles up
- A sense of equilibrium and balance
- Everything feels OK
- Acceptance

This Self is always present. When we drop our preoccupations with our mind stuff, it is here. Many of us can recall moments when we felt utterly complete and in the moment. One way of reminding yourself can be to remember your moments of joy, as in the following activity:

Activity: *Joy moments*

Identify your "joy moments" in your life. Write some of them down, with any recollection of the experience and how you felt:

....
....
....
....
....
....
....
....
....

The goal of a lot of our self-awareness work is to heighten our awareness of this Self. **It is important to direct your awareness deliberately in the desired direction.** In doing this we are undoing habits of a lifetime. The art is to notice the feeling and then to gently keep the attention there, without forcing it. In a sense, just "stay there" with your awareness focused on your feeling. As some say, "God is in the feeling"; you may remember that it is said that love is "the secret sensation of the Self". What you are doing here is to discipline your mind. One way this may be done is to recall a time when you felt full of love or very contented and then to drop the recollection and to stay with the feeling. Again it is the feeling that is crucial.

Activity: *Focusing on good feelings*

You can make this a deliberate practice, to focus your awareness on the present moment and to contact good feelings you have about yourself and the world about you. Give yourself regular time when you sit quietly and just "be" with yourself. Meditation is a good way of doing this, but you can also do this with prayer or with simply being quiet and still. You can be aware of a beautiful place, or pleasant memories, or a person whom you love. Or you could have an object, a picture, a sacred text, an uplifting book or a symbol that you look at that engenders positive feelings. Allow your awareness of the

The Self

feeling to grow and then take that into a meditation or into your quiet time.

Make a note of any ideas that come to mind on reading this:

....
....
....
....
....
....
....
....
....

Maps of consciousness

One way of understanding who you are is to approach it through a study of the understandings of great thinkers. While in this book we have been stressing the importance of your own experience, here we will pause and take a look at what one major contemporary Western thinker and some of his colleagues have to say about the self.

The benefit of this is that it helps give a map to where we are going in our exploration of our own potential.

Ken Wilber

Ken Wilber, who has a passion for integrating ideas from many directions, wrote a book called *The Atman Project*[26] in which he argued that humans evolve through stages or levels of consciousness. Omitting the other lower levels that he describes, certain key stages for our purposes are summarised in the following:

> **i. The Membership level**
>
> Here the self is identified with the family. The individual is none, the family or group is all. The external world is distrusted, if not feared. The past and ancestors are revered. Elders, parents, gurus, leaders know better. Safety lies in obeying the traditions and practices of the group.
>
> **ii. The Mental Ego**
>
> At this stage, the person has achieved a sense of personality and is able to play roles. He has a level of independence apart from the family. He joins in peer and couple bonds but feels himself to be separate. Emotions and thinking are quite sophisticated but there is a lot of self-control. He needs esteem from others. His sense of self comes from a comparison with others. Conditioning is important and he finds it hard to escape from his history. He separates

---

[26] Ken Wilber, *The Atman Project*, Wheaton, Illinois, Quest Books, 1980

intellect from emotions and sees his intellect as residing in the brain.

iii. The Centaur

Here, the person is moving on to start to experience the lessening of the ego's grip. She becomes authentic, genuine. She views herself as being responsible for herself and sees the world through her own eyes and not the eyes of others. She believes that "I create my world", that she creates her own meaning. She has let go of her past. She relates to others from her own centre of experience. Others, like Maslow, talk of this as being the level of "self-actualisation". To Wilber, this is the most individualistic stage. It can be a very atheistic stage.

iv. The Subtle

Here, entering the **transpersonal** realm, the person is aware of experiences that reach beyond the body-mind. He may be aware of psychic phenomena. He finds imagination and intuition to be important. He is letting go of self-autonomy and sees connections with others. He entertains possibilities of other realms of existence. He experiences messages coming from higher or deeper sources. He is inclined more to surrender to experience and may enjoy brief periods of rapture or bliss. Once the individual assessment by the mind is dropped, there is a sense of connectedness. Compassion with others is experienced. Barriers are coming down.

v. The Causal

At this stage, there is a realisation that the current world is an illusion, that there is a higher source with which she is at One. There is no interest in psychophysical phenomena, such as the various beings identified in the subtle phase. There is no ego inflation. Humility is prevalent. Frequent contact with her Source occurs. Death is meaningless since all there is is Consciousness, and it is not limited by the body. Radiance of Being is a constant experience. Love and compassion with others and the world overflows, love being one of the key aspects of the causal. There is true self-transcendence.

vi. Non-dual or ultimate

Complete at-oneness with All That Is. In Buddhism, the Nirvana level; in Yoga *So 'ham*, "I am That"; in the Old Testament of the Holy Bible "I am That, I Am".

As we reach the higher stages, since experience is primary here, words become totally inadequate in attempting to describe something that is beyond words. In fact using words places a limit on something that is limitless.

What is very useful about this way of presenting human evolution is that it presents human kind as having a potential and a will to evolve to higher levels of being, with an expanded sense of lasting contentment.

In his more recent work, Wilber has taken his thinking a lot further[27]. He outlines what he calls an "integral" view of human evolution, presenting his ideas through a model of four quadrants that draws together all human activity. He draws heavily here on the ideas of Clare Graves and of Beck and Cowan[28].

Spiral dynamics

Seeing evolution in terms of Spiral Dynamics, Graves, Beck and Cowan describe evolution as passing through a series of "memes". A meme is considered to be a unit of cultural ideas, symbols or practices and has been applied to stages in evolution. As one moves from one meme to the next, people "transcend and include" (Wilber's words) the previous meme in order to move on to the next. They include the current thinking but transcend it to move on to a higher level. However the first three to be described tend in practice to be very

---

[27] Ken Wilber, *A Theory of Everything*, Boston, Mass., Shambhala, 2000.
[28] Don Beck and Chris Cowan, *Spiral Dynamics*, Boston, Mass., Blackwell, 1995

opposed to one another. (Here the earlier memes are again omitted for reasons of space)

i. The Blue meme: Mythic order

An all-powerful order directs all life, with enforced obedience expected to principles of "right" and "wrong": rigid social hierarchies, paternalistic, a belief in law and order, one right way to think about things, fundamentalist, conformist. This meme is 40% of the world population and has 30% of the power.

ii. Orange: Scientific Achievement

This meme is 30% of the world population and has 50% of the power. This group, typified in the industrialised West, is: individualistic, rational, achievement orientated, materialistic, holds to the primacy of the marketplace, believing in the interplay of interests, and in winners and losers.

iii. Green: the Sensitive Self

This meme is 10% of the population and holds 15% of the power. It is strongly communitarian, stressing feelings, caring, a respect for the earth, anti-hierarchy, relationship, reaching decisions through reconciliation and consensus, egalitarian, a belief in human potential, pluralistic values.

The authors argue that we as a society are poised for a quantum leap into a "second-tier" of thinking which is able to include all the previous memes, while the latter have tended to differentiate themselves from one another and be in conflict. This "second tier" consists of:

iv. Yellow: Integrative

With yellow, 1% of the population, 5% of the power, we have an acceptance of a kaleidoscope of natural hierarchies, systems and forms. Life is one of spontaneity, flexibility, and interdependence, where competence is respected and there is an acceptance of different levels of reality,

v. Turquoise: Holistic

0.1% of the population, 1% of the power. This meme believes in a universal holistic system, where feeling and knowledge are united and multiple levels are interwoven into one conscious system. A "grand unification" is possible in theory and actuality. Everything permeates everything else. This is similar to the Transpersonal levels referred to earlier, in the Subtle areas and above, and is associated with the emergence of a new spirituality, quantum physics, chaos and complexity theory, and so on.

With both these ways of thinking, those of Wilber's levels of consciousness and the later Spiral Dynamics, we can see that there are approaches to human development that envisage humanity's potential to evolve into higher levels of awareness, thinking and experiencing.

Some other thinkers

The various writers in the transpersonal tradition of psychology, James Hillman in the post-Jungian tradition, Psychosynthesis, the Eastern approaches of Buddhism, various gurus in Yogic mysticism, Taoism and Sufism, are other possible examples. An excellent introduction to Transpersonal Psychology and therapy is John Rowan's book, *The Transpersonal*[29].

---

[29] John Rowan, *The Transpersonal*, 2nd edition, London, Routledge, 2005

Ego characteristics

As can be seen in the study of levels of consciousness, growth becomes a process of being more aware and letting go of the hold of the Ego. The Ego as we have noted earlier is the limited sense of "I", in which we identify with what we believe are certain attributes that we possess. We believe this is who we are, but it is an illusion.

We will now examine some of the Ego's characteristics. Part of the process of deepening our awareness of who we really are is to hone still further our ability to discriminate, to spot when our ego is at work, to "**witness**" it. This may take time to learn but with practice becomes a very effective tool. We then cease to identify with aspects of our ego but witness them as objects of perception within our field of awareness. What happens is that aspects of our personality subside and become less active if not inactive, while others awaken and become stronger.

Qualities of the ego

Here now are some characteristics of the small self. What follows is an extensive exercise, **"Knowing your Ego"**, which invites you to reflect more deeply about what occurs for you. Read through this list, spend a little time with each in turn and notice in what ways it manifests in your life.

Some may be obvious, some subtle, some you are not aware of, and some may simply not apply to you. Raising your **awareness** of when some aspect of the small self is at work is one way to gradually free yourself:

Activity: Knowing your Ego

Look through the list of ego characteristics below and make a note to yourself of when you get caught up with any particular characteristic:

Separate

Feeling separate from other people and the world; feeling "different". This is the classic ego experience, the sense of being this particular person, distinct from others, with "good" and "bad" qualities as we perceive them, even alone and isolated.

....
....
....
....

Limited

Both in mind and body; a sense of being limited in what you can accomplish.

....
....
....
....

Wanting

Being motivated by desire: "I want" or "I need"; an awareness of lack, of lacking something; always wanting something that is currently missing. "This is not enough". "There is not enough". Wanting "more". Not content with what is.

....
....
....
....

Fearful

A bottom-line emotion is fear. It may show up in other guises, such as anxiety or worry.

....
....
....
....

Ego characteristics

Constantly thinking

The chatter of the mind, which sustains the small self. Preoccupation with things going on in the mind.

....
....
....
....

Projecting

Projecting positive and negative thoughts and feelings on to others: "That is what they are like, not like me".

....
....
....
....

Living in the future or past

Rather than the present.

....
....
....
....

Problem-focused

Finds and seeks to solve problems in the external world. A belief that happiness is to be found in the external world and therefore that is what needs to be fixed. "When this is sorted, then it will be OK." It would be OK if only other people, situations, the world, life were different. A tendency to put off "being happy" until "the future".

....
....
....
....
....
....

Judgemental

Judges others, self or situations.
....
....
....
....

Comparing

Compares self with others, either favourably or unfavourably. Comparing one situation or set of circumstances as against another. Better or worse; bigger or smaller; richer or poorer; superior or inferior; etc.
....
....
....
....

Doer

A sense of being the doer; having to make things happen, rather than letting go and accepting, allowing or trusting
....
....
....
....

Incomplete

A sense of not having "got there yet", or that something is unfinished. Something is always missing; striving; again anxious; even in spiritual activities. Needs to get things sorted out first. Has not resolved things with people.
....
....
....
....

Ego characteristics

Guilty

At fault; blaming self or others; feels shame or shames others. Being "right"; making other "wrong." May be arrogant towards others. In spiritual matters, seeing God as a judging God, as angry and liable to punish; the need to do penance.

....
....
....
....

Self-importance

Even arrogance: a need to "put self out there" as someone special
....
....
....
....

Self-deprecation

Putting oneself down. Core belief that "I'm no good", "not good enough". "I'm sorry". Not valuing self. Low self-esteem.
....
....
....
....

Resentful

Holding something against someone or something; angry; bitter; complaining; a grudge; hurting
....
....
....
....

Some other Ego manifestations

Here are some other ways that the ego shows up:

Attachment

Holding on to something or some state of being; not letting go. "I must have this".

Aversion

Things we don't like, even hate. What we criticise, condemn, find disgusting. What we can't accept about others.

Attraction

Being attracted to some people, in preference to others, maybe persistently so.

Compulsion

Knee-jerk responses. What we do without thinking. Outside our awareness.

Identification

Seeing the self as the mind or the body (or more!) We identify ourselves with what we think, with our bodies, our experiences, events that happen in our lives, our emotions, even our material possessions and our relatives and friends ("this is who I am; these are mine"). Eg. "I am depressed".

Introjection

Internalised rules by which one lives one's life, taken on board without question from others or society and lacking in choice. "Should", "ought", "must", "got to", "have to", being 'right'.

Addiction

Things we think we can't do without, but which are not basic to our survival

Inhibition

Restraining ourselves. Limiting our self-expression. Holding on.

These are some ego manifestations. As you read through them, you'll probably find yourself thinking of others not on the list.

An interplay within yourself

The small self plays out a constant interplay within itself. To understand the ego is to be aware of when these interactions are going on.

The personality tends to operate in a range of **polarities**, or opposites, and to identify itself with one or other of these polarities. You might be aware in your thinking of how you might have distinguished between things such as good and bad, right and wrong, winning or losing, feeling superior or inferior, comparing me with you, seeing one as a friend and another as a foe. This way of thinking of things in sharply contrasting terms emphasises separation within us and with others.

Sometimes we may experience ourselves as having **different parts** to ourselves, which interact with each other. An example might be a part which is very critical or judgemental, while another part may feel like a victim or a guilty part, or might be a rebel. These aspects of the small self are simply that: aspects. They are also not who we are. But we identify with these aspects and make them "us".

Developing skill

The art is to use witnessing as a skill to help you become aware of when your ego has kicked in, of how you operate. It can also help you learn to discriminate, to know when you are acting out of your small self, when it has got you by the throat. However, once you notice a part of your ego at work, try not to blame yourself, which is more ego stuff! Of course the ego can do this too; one part may give another part a hard time for not "getting it right", especially on the spiritual path. Witnessing is also a tool to use to unhook yourself from your ego: when you are aware you can start to choose to let go.

So, learn with forgiveness, gentleness, humility and compassion. Remember those powerful qualities that we have to help us, which are part of who we really are and where we want to be, such as

- Surrender
- Love
- Gratitude
- Contentment
- Equanimity and equipoise
- Compassion
- Serenity

It is a matter of noticing and of returning to these qualities of the real self, our steady state, our centre of Being.

From Ego to the Great Self

Developing your sense of "I"

With the big list of ego characteristics in the previous chapters, you might well be justified in wondering where we are going if the purpose of this Part to explore the Self. And yet this is frequently what the mind does. We take our awareness intentionally towards our higher self and then – lo-and-behold – the mind has gone off on some trip about itself that takes us nicely back into ego stuff. The fact however that you are aware of this process is a major development. You are aware of yourself: you have stepped back and witnessed the process. Immediately this opens up the chance for re-connection.

So who is this "I" who at one moment is wrapped up in some mental preoccupation and the next is centred in a calm, aware state? One way of exploring this is self-enquiry, *atma vichara*, a contemplative enquiry into the self where we allow our awareness to centre in on the words "I am"[30]. In doing this we start to become very aware that we are, that we exist. In this practice, we repeat over and over the words "I am" and rest our awareness on the immediate experience of being.

In the "small self" way of experiencing "I am", you may think that you are, say, a mother, you are a chemist, you are a certain nationality, you are a resident of....(your neighbourhood), you are...(how you are feeling), you are tall, you are attractive, and so on. You might have an opinion of yourself too, like "I am slow to learn", "I am a good organiser", "I am kind", "I am respected in my community". As we have seen, some might be positive, some negative, but we are well-used to seeing ourselves this way.

---

[30] *Atma vichara* is most famously associated with the philosophy of Ramana Maharshi, an Indian saint of the early 20th Century who lived in Arunachala.

Knowing your inner self

Activity: As you experience yourself right now, who are you?

How would you describe yourself? Be really honest:

....
....
....
....
....
....
....
....
....

In thinking this way, you might be describing yourself as your ego sees you, which is the process of identification described earlier. If you really get into the ego way of operating you'd pretty soon start finding some negative things to say about yourself. And this would be very typical. Most people don't like to deliberately direct their attention in on themselves because it contacts the part of them that does not like themselves or at least parts of themselves. "Oh, I so dislike my nose". In doing this, we don't notice the deeper "I am" in the background.

So just to be aware of those negative self-perceptions, let's write a few down so that when this kicks in you can recognise it

Activity: Negative "I am" statements

Write down all the negative "I am" statements you can think of:

....
....
....
....
....
....
....
....
....

From ego to the great Self

And, remember, this is not who you are. Each time you say negative things about yourself, the world will reinforce it: thought is creative. So, each time you catch yourself going off on a negative trip about yourself, say to yourself, **"This is not who I am. I am more than this"**.

The universal I am

"Know thyself" (in Greek, γνῶθι σεαυτόν *gnōthi seauton*) were the words inscribed over the entrance to the temple of Apollo at Delphi, where the famous sacred oracle in Ancient Greece was located. Many traditions in both East and West from ancient times onwards say that this the most fundamental question of your life: "Who am I?"

A classic line in non-dualist Eastern philosophy, for example, argues that when you become aware, you step outside your ego and contact who you really are. As one being aware, you are the experiencer. And who, it is then asked, is the experiencer? You are. And who are you? Consciousness is the answer. And what is consciousness? That cannot be answered, it is said, because the moment you answer that question you falsify it, by making it an object; you become separate from it. Consciousness, or spirit, cannot be known in the conventional sense. Knowing lies in the realm of duality, subject and object. The "I" has no form. Ancient Hindu sages described the luminous space in which the world arises and subsides and regarded that space as the "I am", something that is timeless and eternal. According to these traditions, although you cannot know consciousness, you can become aware of it as yourself. You can sense it here and now as your very Presence, the inner space within which you have thoughts.

When we step aside from the ego our ground of Being opens up and expands. It is the context in which we experience the small "I am". It is the witness of the small self. When we stop focusing on our feelings, attitudes and qualities, the content of our mind, and focus instead on the simple sense of "I am", we begin to experience a more spacious and shared sense of self that transcends the contents of our ego identity. The direct experience of being the Self is always pure, nonverbal awareness.

Knowing your inner self

Activity: Contemplation

One way to do this is a contemplation, in which you ask yourself, "What is the source of the experience 'I am'?", or "What is the source of my 'I'?", or "What is the source of my feeling of Being?" and listen for the inner, non-verbal answer that emerges in your awareness. As with all contemplation, avoid allowing your mind to start working on it. Simply sit with the awareness, and allow whatever to emerge. Direct your attention to the source. Maybe meditate on it.

What we are doing here is directing our attention deliberately towards our source of Being.

Another step is to now direct your attention towards the feeling of "I".

Activity: Contemplation of "I"

Allow yourself to focus on the word "I". Feel the sensation. Stay with it. Notice, as a witness, and let go of any negative sensation, feelings or thoughts, since these are not who you are. Bring your attention back to "I". Look right at it, hear the sound as you say "I", sense what "I" is like, witnessing your awareness of being "I". If you get diverted, notice that and bring your attention back to "I". Notice what comes up for you.

Write down what you experience.
....
....
....
....
....
....
....

The inner journey

Don't judge what you experienced, whatever that was; that's ego. Just allow it to be. However faint, it is relevant. Don't compare with others and whether or how far they get it; that's ego too. You may need to return to these activities again and again.

There is only one "I am". There is only one source of "I am". This source is within you, within everything around you and in the space between. It is often described as an inner spaciousness, a silence, a stillness, a pervasive Presence, an invisible Light of Consciousness that reveals, sustains and is the whole world. Consciousness is, and knows that it is. From this pure Awareness, the individual experience "I am" arises. For each of us, the pure sense of Being is the same, as it comes from the same one Being.

Perhaps you are now beginning to see why it is so important to be aware of and set on one side those senses of ourselves as the "small, sweaty ego". At the background of our experiencing lies something vastly greater, which lies in all of us and to which we simply need to turn our awareness.

Living as I am

In this expanded space it becomes perfectly natural to experience yourself, life and other people very differently. It is here that people report feeling full of love, where joy and laughter just bubbles up of its own accord, where what needs to be done is done spontaneously and appropriately, where there is compassion towards others who are still struggling with life, and where there is pure contentment.

Most of us have inklings of this experience at times but quickly distance ourselves from it for some reason. Yet it hangs around at the edge of our awareness, saying: "I'm here. You can come and have a look if you want".

Developing your centre of awareness

For those of us who feel drawn to explore ourselves within, it is a powerful impulse, a longing that expresses the soul's hunger. Many have described the discovery of meeting who they really are as an experience of "coming home", where they have always belonged but been away on some very long journey. Hence the "return" can be accompanied by many tears, tears of joy and release. Some writers describe this as a sense of becoming reunited with the whole. It is of course a place we've known all along.

It is one thing to have an insight into the truth of our Being, it is another to develop consistency in being connected with that place. Many describe powerful awakenings to their inner truth, others gentler ones, but very many find it challenging over time to stay there. For one thing there is the pull of the so-called "real" world (which of course begs the question, what is "real"?), another, more likely, is ourselves and our Ego, which we've seen has a powerful ability to pull us back. After all, the ego is all about our survival, and it does just that. This is where the real work begins.

Life happens, and "shit happens", whether you are on a mountain top or in a busy metropolitan street. Wherever you are, your stuff will still come up sooner or later, till you have dealt with it. What most of us look for are ways to stay focused in who we are while getting on with our everyday lives.

There is an old Buddhist saying:

> "Before enlightenment, chop wood and carry water.
> After enlightenment, chop wood and carry water".

So, what will support you in developing your awareness and in staying connected?

Managing your mind: the constant practice

The flow of the mind is a constant process. So, how we manage it is also a constant process. A focus of awareness arises, we attend to it, engage with it, maybe get a result and then move on to another focus. At any moment, our thoughts may kick in with some ego preoccupation. Therefore, witnessing is a constant practice too.

An example

You are driving to work on a busy multi-lane highway. You are in the outside lane overtaking a line of cars. Suddenly, in your rear mirror you see another car right on your rear bumper. Your heart starts to pound, you feel sweaty, you start to feel on heightened alert and you notice how indignant you are feeling at this driver's unreasonableness. In fact as the moments go by, and you can't pull in – and maybe you don't want to – you start to get angry.....

And then, in the nick of time, you catch yourself doing your familiar road-rage number, you take a deep breath, pause your mental flow of gathering rage and preparedness for battle, indicate to pull over, wish a space to appear – which it does – and you get over. You then notice how those feelings have just passed and you are enjoying a sense of calm. None of that mattered one jot, except to your ego. You now are very aware of yourself, and feel a whole lot better.

You've let go all that stuff and surrendered to the moment.

Of course, you may also recollect times when you've got very carried away by some drama. But that is all it is, a drama – and another lesson.

The point is that you exercised your ability **to become aware and to let go**. This is the constant practice. It requires persistent effort.

Practice is important. We are training our minds to operate differently. We are changing age-old habits. The ego likes to get comfortable, so that we can relax our practice and it can get back into control. Then we are back in the grip of our preoccupations. So we need to remember our practice, and make all of our life part of an on-going activity in monitoring our state.

To that we also need to add the support of some other techniques.

The gap

In our example above there was a moment when the driver noticed the gathering drama in the mind. In an infinitesimal moment in the flow of thinking and feeling, there was a momentary pause, at which point the driver was able to notice her mind in action. This gap in the mental flow is always present. Mostly it occurs between awareness of one phenomenon and the next, but these gaps occur in a train of thought. However, with practice in awareness, you can train yourself to become aware of your process as it is happening, so that the gap, however small, can be exploited for awareness.

The gap can be noticed when we breathe. It may seem as if breathing is a constant process. In fact, there is a slight **pause** at the end of an out-breath and, probably, a smaller pause at the end of an in-breath. Many activities have pause-points. A conversation may have a pause. There may be a pause in music. In fact composers write in pauses so that listeners can reflect on what they are hearing. There are gaps between sounds. While we are waiting for something to happen, there is a gap. Most people can feel a moment of boredom or discomfort when there is a pause and look for something to do or think about while they wait. Thus they miss a moment of paradise.

The gap opens up a possibility to sense the awareness of space, of timelessness, of calm, of stillness. You can sense the uprush of joy, in a moment of enjoyment of the pure beauty of the Self "in the moment". Behind the flood of thinking and activity lies the great spaciousness of pure awareness.

The practice is to allow your attention to become absorbed in these gaps. Each time, they open you up to your real Self. With practice these moments can grow.

Developing your centre of awareness

If you sense your mind return to action mode, you can deliberately put it on hold, if necessary by saying to yourself "**stop**", noticing the mind's tendency, and then returning your awareness to the moment.

Physical awareness

One of the most important ways of centring yourself is by using your body. Awareness of your own body is a very "now" activity.

i. Breath awareness

You can attend to your breath. Let's practice it again.

Activity: Breathing

> Right now, allow yourself to take in a few deeper breaths, breathing down into the diaphragm, so to speak, breathing down into your stomach. Breathe into any tensions and breathe them out on the out-breath. Allow yourself to relax. Keep your attention on your breath. Notice the sensation as the breath comes in through your mouth, through your nasal passages, throat, and into your lungs, and out again. Just watch your breathing in this way for a few moments. Just enjoy these moments you are giving to yourself.

You might now like to ask yourself where your mind was during the breathing exercise. Maybe in suspension?

You can practice your breathing whenever you like. After all, you're doing it anyway!

ii. Body awareness

Also, by breathing down into your diaphragm, you were taking your awareness into your body, down towards your **heart centre**, the energy centre or *chakra* associated with love.

Physically, this centre may be felt by placing your little finger at the bottom of the breastbone in the middle. From there about five fingers upwards takes you to, or nearly to, a small dip in the chest. It is probably more sensitive. Those who have become very aware feel it as a very sensitive spot and, even in having their hand a number of inches above the chest, can still feel the energy of that place. This heart centre is often seen as a core awareness place, and it is not the same as your physical heart. Taking your awareness to your heart centre is often seen as a way of accessing your true self which is said to reside there. Why else do we say, "My heart's desire", when referring to what we really want?

Doing this usually takes people within themselves psychologically. It has a deepening effect, and a stilling of mental processes. Classically, this is a route into meditation. It opens up inner space and we can contact our true self, which is often associated with love and the heart.

You might like to try meditating on your heart centre.

Activity: heart meditation

This time, take some deeper breaths to still yourself and bring your awareness within. When you are ready, allow your awareness to then rest in your heart centre. Breathe into that space. Allow yourself to notice whatever sensations are there. If they feel good, and you may need to let go first of any negativity lying around, then allow those pleasant feelings to just be there and keep your awareness focused on those sensations.

Meditate on that space, with those sensations just being there. If they grow, that's fine. Just stay with it. Don't judge anything, even if you don't feel much. Just stay there, not judging, not thinking, just being in your heart, in your centre.

And, when you are ready, take some deeper breaths and come back gently.

Further, to draw your awareness inside your body and keep it there, you are using the body itself to centre you.

Developing your centre of awareness

Activity; Body sensing

Go inside again, using the breath again if necessary. Allow your awareness to be inside your body. Allow yourself to *feel* yourself inside. See if you can feel the blood running through your body. Can you feel it singing through the body? Notice the subtle tingling in the fingers. Notice your heart beating. Sense your whole body as an energy system, fully alive, alert, sensing. Can you hear the blood in your ears? Take your awareness to your limbs. Can you feel them from the inside? Run your awareness down several limbs, noticing the sensation in different places.

Now notice how you feel - different? Don't worry if it doesn't happen straight away. Just keep practising.

The body is one whole energy system, one which extends right out beyond our body into the auric field around the body. You might notice that by standing close to other people and feeling their energy: you are touching their auric field. Some say that we are in reality just pure energy vibrating at a particular frequency. You might even see a light around another person, especially if you de-focus your eyes and yet keep your eyes in their direction.

We tend to identify with the body, making it who we are. In reality, awareness contains the body. The body is not who we are. Being aware of our body, noticing it, as the witness, is another way of coming into the moment, being present and centred.

Witnessing

As you notice yourself in the moment, you are witnessing yourself. Consciousness is aware. You, as consciousness, are aware of you. So, when you are caught up in some drama, in the moment of awareness, you witness yourself in ego mode doing what you do.

The witness is the aware Self, the "already always knowing". It is the silent presence in the background. As you get to know It, in the sense that you become more aware, It has a loving, benign air about it, It does not judge, It passes no opinion, It just sees. It is the space that opens up when thinking is suspended or stilled, when deep feeling passes and stillness returns. It is the gap, It is the breath, It is the body, It is other people, trees, stars, animals, nature and the world around us, witness of us, part of us.

Patanjali, who wrote the *Yoga Sutras*, said, "The mind and its objects cannot be known simultaneously". You cannot be aware of your mind and be thinking thoughts at the same time. Awareness contains thoughts and feelings. Once you become aware of awareness, thoughts and feelings disappear.

Witnessing is pure awareness, a perfect way to centre yourself, a direct access to bliss.

The awareness of the mind is a subtle presence. In fact, some say that this is Presence with a capital P. That's another meditation, on Presence.

You can still get on with life. You are just not caught up in your mind stuff.

Detachment and surrender

When you become skilled at pausing, entering the present, and becoming the Witness, you are more able to be **detached**, to not be "caught up" in the drama, and to **surrender**, to give it up, to let go, to become centred in your awareness again.

Developing your centre of awareness

In centring yourself, you enter a place which some describe as one of equipoise, of balance, of stillness within. As you are no longer engaged in your drama, but rest as the Witness of it, you are in a place of inner stillness. This is never the place of detachment in the sense of indifference. It is an alive detachment, coming from a place of love, of compassion, both towards yourself and towards others. It is not judging, as some fear it is. It is an acceptance, an allowing, a surrender to what is.

Surrender is not an action of weakness, of giving up: it happens because at some level you know what is really needed here. You know you can do this from a place of true strength, an inner strength, a recognition of the Whole. You can do this because you know you can let go of what you do not need, because it does not serve you and because you know divine process will unfold just as it needs it to for your higher purpose – and you are part of divine process. So you give it up. Instead you trust that whatever will be, will be. And then it just works out fine. In fact it is much more likely to work out like that if you let it.

The ego can't bear what you have just read: "That's illogical". It fights for its survival. Surrender is a jump into the void – and the ego is terrified of it, which is why it will fight like mad. And the void contains true peace. As Theolyn Cortens says[31] about Holy Spirit, Ruah ha Kodesh,

> "The Holy Spirit is an Empty Room where all is silent, perfect and complete. It is an Abyss into which we step in faith, knowing that the divine seeks only what is good for us. This room is veiled with a Cloud of Unknowing, but when we surrender to its oblivion, we shall know even as we are known".

True surrender is probably a bit like dying, where we die to the ego in the moment. So we are reminded of our mortality and of our inevitable death, and that in dying we step into the Abyss and are known as we know. No wonder we resist letting go.

---

[31] Theolyn Cortens, *The Angels' Script*, Caer Sidi, UK, 1997

Re-connection

What humans fear most is their separation from the Whole. That underlies all their pain. It is brought up close to us through our fear of the loss of loved ones or through the thought that we are unloved or the fear of being abandoned. The bottom line negative emotion is fear. When you feel fear, you now know what has kicked in. But the truth is we are never separate; there is always love. That is our essence. We think we are separate – that is the great illusion.

When we let go and surrender we find true freedom. It is there all along. This is not legal, political, economic or social freedom, or something obtained by being wealthy. That is the illusion of the ego, of the material world, a function of desire, and no real peace lies there.

So when we surrender, we feel at peace. We feel a sense of **Oneness**. Here is our Centre.

We can re-connect at any time, anywhere, even on crowded subways. In fact try the people experiment. Deliberately do this when you are around others. They are part of you.

Being with other people

Now, take yourself somewhere where you can be with other people. It could be in a café, with friends, with family, in a shop, in the street. Allow your awareness this time to reach out to include others. Allow yourself to feel their presence. Make eye contact if possible. Just be there with these people. Smile at some if you feel like it. They will feel your love at some level and will smile back. Quite normal. Just be present with them. Feel their energy. Sense the enthusiasm of a group of people together. Enthusiasm is from the Greek *enthusiasmos*, *en* meaning "in, within or possessed" and *theos* meaning God. Thus we are "carrying God within". So, as you are there with all those people, allow yourself to feel God in all those people, or whatever other term works for you. As others often tend to be mirrors of you, therefore allow yourself to see yourself in others. As you come to see God in others, so also can you come to see God in yourself. Such is the

Developing your centre of awareness

blessing of being with others. Despite the illusion of separateness, **we are never alone**.

Being present

Part of the constant practice is also to sustain your awareness as much as you are able to. This too is a practice. And when you lose it, know that you have never really lost it - and you can still become aware that you've noticed it, and then bring your awareness back to your sense of who you really are. The more you know who you are, the easier it becomes to return. But it requires an effort of will.

Having an alert sense of your Self is often described as being Present. While many understand that term as being in the moment, if you have the understanding that the Moment is a profound place to be, then Presence takes on a wholly greater meaning.

And you can have that awareness while going about your daily activities. This is very important. We are not talking about an experience reserved for a quiet time by yourself. We are saying this is lived moment by moment in the world, if we choose to.

So a practice is to stay in your centre and be aware of what is going on around you.

Activity: Presence

Allow yourself to become aware of what you understand by your centre within. This might be when for example, what you feel inside when you become aware of the present moment, or when you become still and peaceful, or when you focus on your breathing, or when you go to your heart centre. Just allow yourself to go to that special place, and stay there for a few moments so that you connect with it and allow the sense of Presence to grow in you.

Then, when you are ready, while keeping your awareness within, open your eyes very gently and very softly, and look around you. Notice that part of your awareness that is still focused within but which is also in some contact with the world around you.

Now, go about your daily activities while keeping with you some sense of your centre within.

Write down any awarenesses that come to mind:
....
....
....
....
....

This is practice that you can apply in any of life's situations. What you are doing is intentionally maintaining your contact with your Self while going about life's activities. It can be an anchor when you are in difficult situations or just when you are doing what you usually do. You can still be talking to others, engaged in a physical activity, or very occupied mentally, and yet hold that constant sense of Presence. And, again, if you forget and your ego gets back in control, you can still remember Awareness and return.

I am That

As a final piece let's look at a particular technique for meditation.

This time, we will use the mantra "*So'ham*", meaning "I am That". A mantra is a sacred phrase that is repeated in meditation to act as a focus, to steady the mind, to still the mind, to keep attention on what is uplifting or centring, and to allow the Presence of the Self to manifest itself – depending on which interests you most.

When you go within, using the breath as we have done before, keep your awareness on your breathing for a bit and, when you have stilled yourself enough, then bring in the mantra. The mantra is then repeated over and over again, in rhythm with the breath. In the case of *So'ham*, it is said in reverse and is said as "*Hamsa*". "*Ham*" is the sound of the universal "I". It goes like this:

Developing your centre of awareness

Activity: Hamsa meditation; "I am That"

On the in-breath, say "ham" (sounds like "hum") and on the outbreath say "sa" (like "sar"). So you very gently breathe in to "ham" and as you let your breath go out, you say "sa". Meditate with the sound of the mantra vibrating within.

Imagine, as you breathe in to the mantra, that you are taking your awareness to your heart centre (your heart energy centre or heart chakra is not your physical heart but is to be found, as we have seen, in the centre of your chest, about 4 or 5 fingers above the base of your chest bone). And when you breathe out, you are now breathing from your heart centre out through your nostrils in a semi-circular motion to a place outside you at an approximate level to where your heart centre is, which place is known as the external heart centre.

As you breathe in, allow yourself to become aware of the subtle still point where the in-breath becomes still for an infinitesimal moment before going out. Have your awareness be there. It is another gap, which can grow if you allow it to. With practice you can begin in a very subtle way to get a sense of merging, in a space of supreme stillness, as if you are even becoming "That". The same also applies at the end of the out breath.

Allow yourself to rest in the awareness "I am That".

You can learn more about this meditation in a small but utterly profound book, *"I am That"* by Swami Muktananda[32]

---

[32] Swami Muktananda, *I am That*, SYDA Foundation, South Fallsburg, NY, 1978

Part 4: In the real world

The Real World

Very often people make great learnings on programmes or in coaching but report that very quickly it falls apart in what they refer to as the "real world" outside, in their everyday lives. Then, if we aren't careful, we start to doubt what we've learned and slide back into our old ways. Yet this stage, the application stage, is absolutely crucial. What otherwise is the point of doing the work? This is where you get to practice what you have learned, apply it in real situations and if necessary report back for a review.

What is happening here is that you are unlearning old habits and learning new ones. This takes time and effort. Neurologists have observed that in their studies of the brain, repeat thoughts and feelings have distinct pathways. So, when the "subject" being studied changes these patterns, new pathways gradually appear and the old ones gradually wither away. We literally re-wire our brains. So, no wonder habits take time to change, especially those of a lifetime.

In this part therefore we examine how we apply what we have been learning in the other parts of this book in "live" situations. After all, this is where we get tested. This is the hard bit – doing it every day, every moment, in the so-called "real world".

We say "real", usually to distinguish learning situations from real-life things that happen, at work, in the home, in relationships, in everyday occurrences. Some even go so far as to say that what is real is somehow different from a learning situation. This is at the very least debateable. It can be argued that we are no different in any situation; it is how we respond, how our internal acquired programming kicks in, in those situations. It also begs the question about what is "real" in any case. As you have gathered by now in this book, what is "real" is the reality we choose to create moment by moment. Those so called "real life" situations are just more situations where we make those choices moment by moment.

So, for this part, we will look at certain areas of our lives where these challenges to our growth can often occur.

The real world

We'll start by reflecting on all those situations in daily life where things happen, where some things work out as you would like and others don't.

How do you show up?

So ask yourself, how do I show up in my "everyday life", in all those everyday situations? Where do you get tested? And where does it work?

For example, think about where you get problems with your boss, peers or customers, where you fall out with your partner at home, where there are difficulties in the family, where your buttons get pushed, when you get upset or angry, when you worry, when those old familiar patterns emerge. What works and what doesn't?

Activity: "How do I show up?"

At work
....
....
....
....
....
....
....
....
....
....
....
....

With other people
....
....
....
....
....
....

In the real world

At home

Life in general

In the other parts of this book, a lot has been said about awareness and witnessing, noticing moment by moment when we get caught up in our life dramas and lose our centredness. It is when we are engaged in our lives that we can so easily lose our connectedness. This is really where we need self-discipline and sustained focus on what we are about. Every moment holds a gift in its hand: we can continue "outside of awareness" or we can re-member, witness our behaviour,

The real world

re-mind ourselves of who we are and then return to a place of calm. This is the practice.

So, in this part of the book, we will use the principles discussed in the other parts and apply them to several common aspects of our everyday lives. But first we will draw attention to four key supports as we go about living our lives, **will, trust, purpose and intention.**

Will

In choosing to shift our awareness into more positive pathways, we start to mobilise our resources for action. Here we are making use of our will. It is a conscious use of the power of the mind.

In terms of making changes, this can be a crucial stage in harnessing the potential in awareness. People often fail to act on their awareness. Somewhere they lack willpower to make the change. Somehow it seems easier to stay put. We call this being in "comfortable discomfort"! It seems easier to continue in the old familiar but unsatisfactory ways. This is often because making the change seems more threatening than the status quo. To step across the threshold into a new way of being might be very scary. It is not always easy to see that actually the result might be a breakthrough.

Thus people don't like to **commit**. They might prefer to procrastinate, to put off taking the step. This is very common at the moment, people shopping around trying out different paths, looking for the quick fix but reluctant to actually take the really powerful step that will move things on. It involves facing the fear, since fear is frequently at the bottom of all this. It involves making a decision and fundamentally committing. Will power is vital here.

Somewhere inside you will know you want to do something. When that is sufficiently strong, you'll be more inclined to act. Then you will tap into your will.

It can be useful to be aware of this process in a bit more detail.

As you have seen, there is a process we can go through to let go of what is not useful for us and shift our awareness on to what we would prefer. Thus we become aware of what we are doing, we step into the Awareness gap in the mental stream of thoughts, we notice what is happening through witnessing it, we pause, we take responsibility for our experience, we choose, we let go of what we don't want and we focus our mind on what we prefer. Taking responsibility and making a choice involves the will. We are willing to act.

Will

The psychotherapy of Psychosynthesis emphasises the use of the will. Will Parfitt[33] says that an act of will goes through 6 steps:

1. Investigation (finding out what we wish to do)
2. Deliberation (selecting the acts most relevant)
3. Decision (deciding on the most relevant act right now)
4. Affirmation (staying connected with this decision through constantly reaffirming the choice)
5. Plan (Ways to do it)
6. Execution (doing it)

We have already stressed in this book how important it is to choose, decide, affirm and act.

He goes on to say that there are 4 levels to willing:

i. **Having no will**: this is where we feel a victim to circumstances, where we think we have no choice. This is the most disempowering place to be. The way out of this involves us in seeing that we create our experience every moment and are the true author of our actions.

ii. **Will exists**: we realise we have a choice. We then need to build up our will. This involves the strong will, the energy to choose, and skilful will, the knowledge of how to use that energy. Will Parfitt speaks of bringing choice into a regular part of our everyday life so that we have increasing awareness and confidence in it.

iii. **Having a will**: we start to take responsibility and act with purpose. It is a conscious act.

iv. **Being will**: we become connected to our inner-most understanding. We become the cause of what happens in our life. We act according to our higher purpose.

---

[33] Will Parfitt, *The Elements of Psychosynthesis*, Shaftesbury, UK, Element Books, 1994.

Activity: Developing your will

In what areas of your life do you lack willpower?
....
....
....
....
....

What will you commit to doing to exercise your will in these areas?
....
....
....
....
....
....
....

People often have weak willpower, as has been said already. Thus they fail to follow through and act on their awareness. They need to build their will so that it becomes the powerhouse that they can really use to make a difference. As has been pointed out, a lot of this is due to fear, the bottom-line emotion that holds us back. We discussed these resistant emotions in Part 2 of the book. It is also useful however to appreciate that we may also fail to act on our awareness because of other subtle resistances centred on trust.

Trust

Having summoned up the will to take another course of action, you might think that it is now quite simple. "Just do it". However, there is a subtle distinction to be made here. You will also need to trust in what you are about to do.

Trust, faith and belief in self are such an important part in **confidence**, the inner faith in our Self and in our ability to act.

People often find that when they are reading material like this, or taking part in a programme in a group, they feel more confident and supported on their path. The real difficulties occur, as we have seen, when they are on their own, having finished the programme, when they are carrying out their daily activities in life, at work, or at home. Then doubts kick in and they are more prey to their egos. They become less inclined to take the steps that they have learned are useful for them if they are to grow. This is often where trust comes in.

How much do you trust?

"You just need to let go and trust", they say. This sounds ever so simple and yet can be difficult to do. Trust goes against everything the Ego has learned. The ego thinks we are unsafe, that the world is a threatening place, that we had better be careful. To the ego, we have to work hard to keep on track. To let go and trust is anathema. The small child trusted but somehow, maybe by 7, we became suspicious and wary: the 7 to 8 year-old is more aware of being separate and needing to establish his or her sense of self, and they start to be more careful in relationship to others. Then as we grew up, we discovered the reasoning mind and instead tried to rationalise it out. Trust and reason do not sit easily together.

Not to trust is one of the greatest barriers on the path. Not to trust is to "get what we've always got", so to speak.

The curious thing is that many of us still trust quite a lot. You might care to check in what parts of your life you trust without thinking.

There are those, for example, who think nothing of standing looking over the edge of precipices, or who will drive a car fearlessly or take big jumps over streams knowing they will reach the other side safely. In a more mundane way, we take risks knowing somehow that we will be OK, such as crossing a road knowing that somehow we'll get across safely, while others might be petrified in case a fast car roars around the corner and knocks them over.

Activity: When do you trust?

In what situations do you trust?
....
....
....
....
....
....
....
....
....

It is a choice

In trusting, we take a step in certain belief that we are safe, unquestioning. It is a state of surrender, a letting go. We may do it in calm confidence. If we are worried as we act, we are not trusting. To trust is to act in the belief that we will be OK. The questioning ego is in suspension.

So, to walk the path we are talking about in this book, trust is part of the process. We are not going to get there unless we trust, because the shift to another dimension requires trust. We notice our fears, witness them, let them go, and take action. And we keep on with our actions, even when fear kicks in. Fear is not who we are. Fear is ego; it is False Evidence Appearing Real, an illusion. We discussed fear in the second part of this book. It is the great under-miner of all our efforts. Fear attracts: it attracts what we fear. Have you noticed how when you are anxious about something, you end up getting what you are anxious about? And at the bottom, really at the bottom, is the fear of no love, of separation and of death. Trust moves us in another direction, where we let go and make a shift towards a stiller, more centred place, from which we act with confidence, creatively, knowing we are OK.

From trusting to knowing

Learning to trust means learning to step into and live from our centredness. It is part of the process of learning how to be. It is part of learning about our place of boundless love, our inner certainty.

Let's look at the car park phenomenon. You might know people who talk of creating car parking spaces by thinking in advance that there is a car park space that is vacant when they arrive. In such an approach, they are stepping into their own "inner parking place" of knowing, and are therefore acting from their most powerful creative space. They are "intending" that there is a car park space. If they allow doubt to creep in, they are not in that space any longer and there is no parking space "out there" for them.

In the Greek myth of Orpheus and Eurydice, Orpheus had just married his sweetheart, Eurydice, when she had been bitten by a snake, had died and been taken to the Underworld. Orpheus could not accept his loss and had journeyed to the Underworld and begged Pluto, the ruler of the Underworld, and Proserpine that she be returned to him from the Underworld. This wish was granted on condition that as the two journeyed back to the land of the living, he did not look back at her. However, on their way back, in a moment of forgetfulness he looked back to see if she was still following him, and he lost her.

To trust is to truly let go of doubt and fear, to take **courage**, to believe that it will be OK. Courage is of the heart, our centre of inner strength and love. It is from here that we act creatively, as author of our lives.

As we have seen, a further step beyond believing is knowing. As we learn more to approach life from a state of Being, of knowing who we are, we can BE the place where we want to be. It is a shift of perspective. Then we can move beyond trusting, because, since everything from a perspective of Being is perfect just as it is and all

In the real world

part of the One, whatever occurs is just right and we, in that place just accept it. Fear is not present, nor is effort. It just is. When we truly know, we've moved beyond needing to trust.

Trusting takes us down the path of learning to let go and believe, and the more we get to know it works the more we can let go even of needing to trust.

So, learning to trust is part of the practice of becoming the centred being you really are.

Activity: Practice trusting

Think of areas of your life where you could trust more in order to make something happen or to achieve something or carry out some part of your normal life. Where do you have difficulty trusting? Practice it here.

....
....
....
....
....
....
.

Having vision and purpose

TS Eliot wrote at the end of his final and arguably greatest set of poems *The Four Quartets*[34], in the final poem *Little Gidding*,

> We shall not cease from exploration
> And at the end of all our exploring
> Will be to arrive where we started
> And know the place for the first time

He seems to suggest that at the end of the journey of life we come to truly know the Source. It is also a metaphor for self-development, that at the end of that journey we come to some sense of truth of who we are.

As we saw in the first part, Viktor Frankl, the author of *Man's search for Meaning* regarded humans as meaning-seeking creatures who needed purpose. It was this that enabled some to survive Auschwitz. To have purpose is to have an object, aim or intention. If you follow a path, you presumably intend to get somewhere. You probably have some idea of what that goal is.

For many, the current age is one of seeking. There is a pervasive sense that what we have, in an age of unprecedented affluence, is unfulfilling. Something is missing. People therefore need a sense of higher purpose to help them define themselves, one that is uplifting and motivating. Of course, it might be said that when the goal has been achieved, purpose becomes unnecessary as we are in a state of desirelessness. Until then, it is useful.

For self-development, it is powerful to choose a vision or purpose that will give direction to your efforts. Remember the power of the mind, its creativity. What we think, we are. What occurs in our life is our choice. Therefore we need to think what we intend.

---

[34] TS Eliot, *The Complete Poems and Plays of TS Eliot*, London, Faber, 2004

Visioning the life you want

What do you really want? What life do you wish to create? In particular, what would most represent your higher purpose?

Activity: Your higher vision

A useful exercise is, in your mind's eye, to take yourself to age 85, let's say, and look back on your life. What do you regret not having done? Do you feel contented about your life? Do you really feel you achieved what was most important for your soul's purpose? Give yourself time to go inside and explore this.

....
....
....
....
....
....
....
....
....

Activity: Your purpose. What do you want?

Then get a pen and paper and go somewhere quiet for a short while. Take a meditative posture, breathe deeply, relax, and go inside. Become still. Now ask yourself, "**What do I really want as my life's purpose?**" Breathe, and just allow whatever is there to emerge, without forcing it. Check it, like we did with focusing in the first part. See what feels true, what it tells you, how it looks, what is inspiring, what gives you a lift, even a little one like "this makes sense". Come back and write it down.

....
....
....
....
....
....

Having vision and purpose

....

If you like, you can meditate on this regularly, and let things emerge and make themselves clearer. Spend time with this and add to it as more comes to mind. You might find you need to change it.

Most visioning of this kind needs to be specific and relate to every area of your life, the more so because you are setting a powerful intention. And remember, what you think....happens. Thought is creative.

It can be tricky, since we often write material outcomes, when the truly fulfilling goal has more to do with fulfilment. The trap of the material is that it is impermanent: in the world of the Ego, all is impermanent; nothing ever stays the same; change is a constant. The material goal does not satisfy enduringly, and those who have material goals find that when they've achieved them, they wonder what else they want next, endlessly going round the cycle of wanting. It is well-known for successful business people to create major organisations and amass personal fortunes, and then still feel unfulfilled. So, tread with care and discrimination.

We also tend to set goals as something in the future. You might try writing your vision statement again in the present tense, as something that already exists. While that might sound crazy for something that is future-related, what we are doing is telling our unconscious self that it is happening.

We may set goals that are really hazily future-related. That is we think that "sometime in the future this is how I'll be", in effect not living like that now and putting off manifestation. So you need to sincerely commit to your vision.

So, decide who you are and get on with working towards it, aided by intention.

Living intentionally

Intention is a very powerful technique. Wayne Dyer[35] defines intention as not just a strong purpose or aim but also a determination to produce a desired result. He says that intention is a force that exists in the universe as an invisible field of energy. By setting an intention, and therefore by positively utilising the field of energy, you set up a path for its attainment and you draw what you intend to you. As Lynne McTaggart[36] has shown, scientists are now finding through their research that the universe at its most basic consists as a complex set of interdependent and indivisible relationships. Hal Puthoff for example calls it the Zero Point Field, "a kind of self-regenerating grand ground of the universe". When we set intentions with deep purpose we resourcefully use this field. When we function out of our egos, we use this force negatively. Once you tap into awareness and exercise intention, creative thinking, you connect with the positive power of the universe.

We need to live from the part of us that connects to the Source. Hence, in setting and sticking with intention, we need to be aware that intention is not sheer brute determination regardless of higher things. Here are some useful criteria you might like to consider:

---

[35] Wayne Dyer, *The Power of Intention*, Carlsbad, CA, Hay House, 2004
[36] Lynne McTaggart, *The Field: the Quest for the Secret Force of the Universe*, London, Harper Collins, 2001. See also the DVD's *What the Bleep do we know*, 2005, and *The Living Matrix*, 2009.

Having vision and purpose

1. It states a concrete outcome.

Good visioning means describing what your life will be like when you get there, in very clear, concrete, detailed terms. And, remember, thought is creative. So you are already putting it out there as something that is going to happen.

2. It inspires you.

You have written it from the depths of your being. It draws you to it. It is impelling. Every time you look at it, you say, "Yes, that is truly what I want, from the depths of my soul". It motivates you.

3. It comes from your higher self.

Something deep inside says, "Yes, that's me". It is as if something would truly be missing if you did not do it.

4. You commit to act from the place you envision.

It is particularly powerful to act as if you are already where you aspire to be. Start doing it. That's a great test of commitment. Following on from this, consider again what we said about intentions as creative forces. In setting intentions you are connecting to higher power. In implementing your vision, what are your intentions for various aspects of your life? How about planning this right now?

What we are doing with intention is creating what is good and beneficial in our lives. Intention needs to have higher purpose in it. In setting intentions, we also need discipline, to stick to our purpose, but additionally patience and surrender, since the universe has a way of getting there in unexpected ways and may not necessarily do it when or how we want. To be attached to your outcome is a behaviour of the Ego, meaning "I must do this" or "My survival is at stake" or some other impulsion that comes from fear, anger or separation.

In the real world

Examples of intentions

You will want to set your own intentions that relate to your own situation and aspirations. Here are some typical intentions, just to get you thinking. The important point is to state them in the present tense, as if they are actually happening. What you are doing is calling the universe in to manifest what you intend. Dyer stresses that it is most powerful to think as if you are already where you want to be.

This example was for someone who decided to change his lifestyle, after having neglected his work-life balance for many years:

"I intend to:
- Meditate daily, each morning before I start my daily activities, for 40 minutes
- Take exercise five times a week by taking regular very energetic half-hour walks
- Eat a healthy diet, and drink moderate amounts of alcohol only at weekends
- Participate in a group activity where I meet people and engage in something that interests me (he's got to go out and create this interest and start meeting people)
- See a friend every week."

Anyone who has neglected themselves for many years will know that in practice this can be hard work, since it involves changing deep-rooted, old-established habits. He therefore had to think about how he would support himself, and get support, to stay on track.

We will look further at aspects like support, commitment and staying on track.

It is possible, however, that you may be challenged in carrying out your intention and, as we have seen, you will need to stick with it to see it manifested. Intentions are all the more powerful when they are directly tackling some area of our lives where we need growth and change and where we truly want to make a difference for ourselves. That is often where the challenges will come. You can for example

Having vision and purpose

find you encounter the opposite to what you intend. Neale Donald Walsch says

> "In the absence of that which you are not, that which you are, is not." [37]

Once you make a stand for something that you are in the world, he says that you are also in effect deciding what it is that you are not. The law of the universe is that a vacuum is created when this occurs, and the vacuum will be filled by "that which you are not". A common way this shows up is when you start to be more yourself in the world, be more authentic. What can happen to begin with is that you meet people who are not like that or encounter situations where you may feel tempted to be inauthentic to get by. So you may get what you didn't intend. He says stick with it and stay on purpose, face the challenge and it goes away.

This means using awareness, the present moment, taking responsibility and exercising choice in recognising those parts of your ego that have popped up to try to pull you back into what it thinks is safe.

Activity: Setting intentions

Now start developing your own intentions

Lifestyle (eg. Work/life balance; how you will spend your time; quality of life)

....
....
....
....
....
....
....

---

[37] Neale Donald Walsch, *Applications for Living*, UK edition London, Hodder and Stoughton, 1999; p. 278

In the real world

Relationships (partner; family, friends, social life)
....
....
....
....
....
....
....
....

Health, diet and exercise
....
....
....
....
....
....
....
....

Job/Career (If you are retired, your main focus of interest)
....
....
....
....
....
....
....
....

Interests
....
....
....
....
....
....

Spiritual life
....
....
....
....

Having vision and purpose

Aspirations (things you want to create in your life; new directions; new adventures)

....
....
....
....
....
....

Miscellaneous

....
....
....
....
....

It is suggested that you put your intentions somewhere where you will regularly look at them and remind yourself of what you intend. Keep your thinking regularly focused on what you intend. But don't be attached to it. Give it freedom: be willing also to let go of it. That is not to say that you give up the intention; it is that you are not emotionally attached to it. The skill is to intend it and not be invested in the fear of it not happening. We will cover the skill of detachment too, later.

This is powerful stuff, which needs revisiting to really imbed the idea and practice it. Many people can be sceptical that they can actually create what they want, or at least they might enthusiastically sign up for an intention while inside them a part doubts it. It challenges old belief systems. Thus they might need to work on their beliefs. Otherwise their powerful creativity might get engaged in not making it happen. This is very frustrating for people who are trying to manifest what they want. They may need to delve deeper and explore and challenge the part of themselves that is getting in the way of making something happen.

Coming from deep purpose

The vision and purpose we are talking about is nothing less than a way of being and living where you are successfully dealing with the limitations of the Ego, where you are fulfilling your life's purpose in manifesting your highest vision of who you are. This is deep purpose: it needs to inspire and motivate, even when the going is tough, as it can be at times. So check that your intention is aligned with deep purpose.

With other people

A lot of people I meet on personal growth programmes or work with in coaching are single or are struggling with their relationships. For them, this is the one big area where they need to do some work. For them securing a good personal relationship is usually a key goal.

It can sometimes seem as if we are each just "an island unto ourselves" and as if other people are an inconvenience which gets in the way. I remember when as a teacher, some staff used to say that the school would be great if it wasn't for the kids. Frustrated people in relationships say that when they are feeling particularly mad, they feel they would be much better off on their own. People on personal growth paths often say that their greatest challenges are their relationships.

Relationship as the highest practice

Relationship, however, holds a special meaning. It is arguably one of the most powerful ways in which we get to experience and confront the illusion of separation, and learn about being connected. When we work on our relationships with other people, we are working on how we keep ourselves separate, alone and disconnected from Oneness. To feel in love with another is one extremely powerful way in which we can experience Oneness. This way of experiencing connectedness is like the other ways discussed in this book, always available. It occurs wherever and whenever we meet other people. It is up to us to open our hearts.

The Shadow

A key principle here is that our relationship with others is also a relationship with ourselves. What we play out with others is our own life drama. We've created the perfect cast with which to enact this play: our partner, our parents, our children, our boss, our neighbours, all obligingly fulfilling their part. They are all part of the field of

In the real world

awareness. These people are all mirrors of parts of ourselves. They are truly parts of us, as we are of them.

To find answers to how we are with others, we need to look within and know our shadow self.

Activity: Knowing your shadow

Describe someone you admire and someone you have a problem with; identify their characteristics or their qualities:

(a) Someone you admire:

....
....
....
....
....
....

(b) Someone you have a problem with:

....
....
....
....
....
....

How much are these people reminding you of a quality in you that you do not fully own or are not comfortable with? If you have a particularly sharp reaction to this quality, it is possible that this is some aspect you do not own. Others might say to you, "but you are like that", and inside we squirm with discomfort.

What happens is that we **project** on to other people aspects of ourselves. It is part of the function of perception described in the second part of this book, our internal filter screens. Sometimes we might catch ourselves doing it. A lot of the time, however, it is outside our awareness.

With other people

Activity: Where you come in

Look back over what you wrote in the previous activity and also what you have written about yourself in other parts of the book, especially in "Becoming Aware". Where are there reminders of you in these people?

....
....
....
....
....
....
....

Often there is a pattern or consistency in the characteristics that come up

The pioneering psychologist Carl Jung called this phenomenon "The Shadow".

We tend to attack each other in our and their shadow areas. This is often where the drama of relationship is acted out. Disowned aspects of ourselves are projected on to our partners and we have a problem with some of those projected qualities. They tend to be polar opposites. What is needed with the Shadow is honesty and humility, and letting go of our ego attachments to being right/better/superior/the winner: "Yes, I too may be like this". Our partners are perfectly chosen to teach us. We need to accept our partners as our teachers and learn from being with them. The same can apply with previous partners.

With the Shadow, these qualities need to be brought out into the open, looked at and acknowledged. Then we can choose to have more or less of them in our lives for ourselves. As with other awareness work, it can free us up.

The classic example of the Shadow in relationship is the loud, dominant, talkative, expressive, flamboyant person and his partner who is quiet, introverted, controlled, considered, and polite. The "loud" one maybe has to learn that being gentle and still is also effective and also gives space for others to own themselves and to step forward. People may then find they are more comfortable around this person. For the partner, it is to step more into being outspoken in her views, to say honestly what's on her mind, to go for what she wants in life and no longer hold back. Both have something important to teach each other. If they can each give the other space, listen to them and respect their right to grow, much can be achieved.

Working with your shadow can be particularly uncomfortable and I think often people find it so uncomfortable that they just don't want to go there. I think they miss out as a result on a crucial aspect of their development. I've so often seen how the shadow aspects of relating have shown up in groups, particularly where there has been conflict between people. In Gestalt Therapy, people are encouraged to own their shadow in relation to another, to acknowledge that which they are projecting on to another. In turn the facilitator may also ask the one who has been on the receiving end of the projection what the "grain of truth" might be. This is because it takes two to make this happen. So the recipient might in turn be able to own some element of the projection. For example, where one person has said she finds another "bossy", she is then asked to explore how she too might have a "bossy" side to herself. The other person in turn might then ask himself whether it is true that he might have a "bossy" side to himself that he does not really let out for people to see.

Ken Wilber has argued that one of the great contributions of Western psychology to spirituality has been the discovery of the Shadow. He suggests that lengthy practice in meditation in Eastern spiritual practice can still fail to get to some of the major ego manifestations in the personality. No wonder it is possible to meet long-term, sincere and dedicated spiritual seekers with a lot of stuff going on in themselves that they don't see. He thus stresses the importance to determined seekers of "finding, facing and re-owning the most feared and resisted parts of ourselves"[38].

---

[38] Ken Wilber, *Integral Spirituality*, Boston, MA, Shambhala, 2006.

A failure to engage with the Shadow is one reason why seekers are reluctant to face and live in the "real" world. For them, there's too much that's nasty going on "out there". To adopt that attitude is to neglect the Shadow at work, except that as shadows do, it follows you around and you continue to get what you resist.

Making others responsible

Relationship is also however, often the perfect example of the blame game, where we make others responsible for what occurs in our lives. So rather than blame each other, we need to look to ourselves and at what illusion we are creating.

Making others responsible is often something that we learned as children. It seemed as though things happened to us and people were responsible for us. When we transgressed, we were blamed and told we were wrong. So it is not surprising that many of us grow up thinking that others are responsible for what happens and they are definitely in the wrong. Things continue to seem to happen "out there" in the world and we seek our solutions to our dilemmas out there.

As we have seen, from the perspective adopted in this book we are responsible for our lives; we are creating it. When things seem to go wrong, it is in truth us that are creating what occurs and we can change it. Making a decision to look at ourselves and the world from this perspective is one of the most profound and decisive shifts that can be made on your growth path. It will liberate your relationships.

But it takes a lot of working on. Our partners have an uncanny knack of knowing just which buttons of ours to push and then – bang! – we are back "on it", blaming the other person. What is needed here is to recognise that a button has been pushed and that we are blaming another for what is in reality our own hurt. This is where we need to notice what is happening and take responsibility for the hurt. You might then be surprised to find your partner also acknowledging their part in what happened. But don't expect it!

Activity: When you blame others

What people or situations crop up in your life where you blame others? Write them down. Then practice letting go of blame with these people or situations.

....
....
....
....
....
....
....
....
....
....

Try being honest with them instead! Honesty is a powerful aid to reconnection. When you own something that you do in a relationship, when you own it with humility, and when it comes from the heart, people truly get it.

Love and needing love

As we saw in Part Two, we can easily confuse love and need. Most of us get into relationship for love – unless of course you live in a culture where it was arranged. But it is not always clear that underlying that love is a deep unmet need to be loved, a "deficit need". The recognition that we are in relationship for the need of love is an uncomfortable realisation. It is common, and also hard to notice.

People want a partner in their life because they feel love is missing unless they have a loved-one. This thinking is based on the deficit need that "I lack love". What people are in truth searching for "out there", is someone who will love them. They may well of course love them back. But it is worth asking the question. Are you in relationship because you need to be loved by someone? Do you fear not being loved? One way this may occur is when your partner is at times apparently not there for you and you feel an upset, like they have

With other people

abandoned you? Then you feel angry and upset with them until they assure you they love you. And you might relentlessly continue in this vein, because things keep happening which "make you" think they don't love you, or that you fear they don't. The deficit need is hard at work.

Needing love is the experience that something might be missing. It is a gap, a fear, a pain. It is based on our own childhood fear of aloneness and separation, from our parents and from the Whole. Love, however, is warm, glowing, filling up our hearts, full of joy, blissful, generous, trusting, compassionate, and unconditional.

As St. Paul wrote in *The Holy Bible*,

> "Love is patient, love is kind. It does not envy, it does not boast, it is not proud. It is not rude, it is not self-seeking, it is not easily angered, it keeps no record of wrongs. Love does not delight in evil but rejoices with the truth. It always protects, always trusts, always hopes, always perseveres. Love never fails." [39]

Love is our very nature and we do not <u>need</u> another to experience love. We can enjoy the wonderful opportunity to love another as a way of experiencing our true nature. But it is not the only way, as for example the devout celibate, the dedicated missionary, the one who commits his or her life to service, or the spiritually awakened have found. Love is within us, not created by another on whom we are dependent in order to experience it. If it depends on another or on certain circumstances, it can become conditional.

This realisation too can liberate your relationships.

---

[39] *The Holy Bible*: 1 Corinthians 13:4, New International Version, New York, 1978

Fear-based relating

Being in an ego-based relationship is to live with part of us withheld, because we fear something might happen. Remember, the ego is about survival and self-protection. This is fear-based, the opposite of love.

Here are some examples:

- **Co-dependency** in relationship is a common condition, where both support each other in some dysfunction. It is often seen in couples who are both alcoholic or have some other addictive behaviour. Both are supporting the other in avoiding a truth.
- **Security**: "If I have you, I'll be alright", where a person is in fear of the alternatives to being with a certain person. The relationship is providing the person with a sense of security.
- **Fear of intimacy**: The reluctance to get close to someone or to let people in; "I'll not let you get close to me".
- **Distrust**, where we will never give all of ourselves for fear of the consequences.
- **Emotionally disconnected**: It is very common to find people who cannot really be all of themselves. They hide themselves emotionally, not disclosing all their true feelings, or not expressing them, or even not being aware of their feelings. Here, they are closed off to their partner.

There is a phrase for intimacy: "Into me see", which suggests that we allow another to see all of who we are. Potentially what one might see in "me" is goodness, wholeness and love without end. And love is trusting, as we have seen.

Patterns of relating: Seeing the rackets

To work on your relationship is, as we have said already, a spiritual practice. We choose our relationships perfectly. Our partners are reflecting back to us some key life lesson we need to learn. You can of course walk away. You always have that right. But you will probably find another with whom you still have to learn the lesson, either in the same form or its opposite polarity. Such is life in the world of illusion, of opposites.

This is an excellent way to practice witnessing, of seeing what your ego is getting up to. Notice your patterns of relating, what Eric Berne calls "the games people play". In relationship we slot into patterns, which Berne calls **rackets**. They are mutually interlocking. We learned them from our parents in some way and we play them out with our partners - or with our parents, children, work colleagues or even friends. Notice how you feel when your buttons are pushed. This time choose not to react but instead feel the feeling, notice what it is about and then work towards letting it go. You might need to really do some work with yourself before you can easily let go, because these sorts of feelings can be fundamental.

Activity: Witnessing your relationship patterns

Here is a chance for you to think of where you get into rackets with your partner, relative, friend or work colleague. Try and think of situations which keep occurring, particularly where you find your buttons get pushed, where you feel a lot, or the other person does. Write down the sequence of events and see if you can find what in you gets stirred up: ask yourself what that is about.

....
....
....
....
....
....
....
....
....
....
....
....
....
....
....

Healing wounds

When we own our part in what occurs in our relationships, we are often in the end contacting deeper wounds within us, which are very historic but continue to play themselves out in our current relationships and dog our lives. We need to own the wound and release ourselves from the **attachment** we have to the feeling, thought, belief or pattern. What is meant by attachment here is the way we can hang on to a negative thought, for example, as if it is attached to us or we to it, so that we won't let it go. Letting go of attachments like this can be painful work for some, where a lot of anger and grief comes up, as they own the pain behind the pattern.

One who is healing an old hurt often needs to **forgive** somebody, to express the pain, take responsibility for it and then seek to let it go. Sometimes this involves a **completion**, where things need to be said or done, where something is brought to an end, so that a person can move on. We have already drawn attention to the book *"Radical Forgiveness"* by Colin Tipping in the second part of this book", which looks at a lot of this material.

It may be increasingly obvious that, in healing old wounds like this, we are not only improving our relationships immeasurably, we are also significantly improving our lives as a whole. What a lot could be done if large numbers might do this! What a transformation of life on the planet, because we also play this stuff out in organisations, in politics and between communities, cultures and nations.

Changing your ways of relating

So, a practice might be to look at how you relate to people in general. Using the awareness skills we discussed in the first part of this book, you might practice for example some of the following:

   a. **Attending to others**: your "social radar". Develop your awareness of other people. How attuned are you to them, their feelings, moods, attitudes, beliefs?

With other people

b. **Being present**: being right there, in the moment, with the other person, fully sensing and feeling, both of what is happening in you, what might be happening in them and what goes on between the two of you.

c. **Listening and hearing**: what the other person is saying, how they say it, what they perhaps don't say, how they look, their eyes, what you sense in you as they say it.

d. **Awareness of your own inner dialogue**: noticing what is going on for you. What are your thoughts and feelings? What are you uncomfortable about? What do you need? What are you resisting? What is getting in the way for you?

e. **Honesty**: Be truthful with yourself and with others, the latter being the scary bit since you will be risking their unfavourable response. Sharing how you feel, in ownership. Making a clear communication: open, honest, direct.

f. **Being non-judgemental**: not making a judgement about another. Giving up having an opinion about another or about some aspect of their behaviour. Not making them wrong.

g. **Accepting**: accepting people for who and what they are, rather than say wanting to change them or make them more like you.

Looking for the jewel

Swami Chidvilasananda, a guru in Maharashtra, India who is also known as Gurumayi, said of relating, "See God in each other". To transform relationship involves not only taking responsibility and healing our own wounds but also taking a good look at our attitude towards others. In others are ourselves. They are us. We are One. So, see the divine in others. In doing so, you will need to own and look beyond your projections and your own stuff which you put "out there" on to others.

Activity: Looking into the eyes

One way of practising this is to get used to looking into people's eyes. The eyes are "the windows to the soul". This is one way we get to practice "into me see". Looking into another's eyes involves accepting that they too will see into you. So you need to practice being aware of

In the real world

and moving beyond your projections, what is part of you which you put on to another, and also accepting what is in you. So you respect and value another and you do the same for yourself. It is something beyond the ego.

As you do this, you may experience a softening, both in you as you let go but also in the other, as if you start to see something vulnerable, tender. This might change moment by moment, as another projection comes in, or more feelings. Or you might just see eyes looking at you and not feel anything.

Just stay with the gaze, or gazes if you are doing lots of little "looks", and notice it when you soften and contact the loving part of yourself. If you start to look from that space, you may well find it gets reciprocated, with a flash or a twinkle and almost certainly a smile. That's when you start finding the jewel. There's a sense that you've really "met" the other person, heart to heart.

When we start to really connect with other people, coming from our hearts, in contact with our own centre, everything with other people somehow gets so much easier. This is beyond our egos, unconditional, at-one, because love is at the essence of relating.

Hence, relationship is a spiritual practice. It brings you into contact with your Self.

What might you start doing differently in your relationships?

....
....
....
....
....
....
....
....
....
....

Work, money and career

Personal growth frequently stimulates people to think about their values, goals and direction in life and thus about reviewing and possibly changing job or career. Parallel to this, but not necessarily as a result, they also find themselves addressing their challenges around money and wealth.

We have already seen how important purpose is. If you have already come up with a statement of purpose that includes what you hope to do to fulfil that purpose, you are probably also making a statement about your chosen direction. If you haven't, you may find it helpful to include your career in your thinking.

Work and vocation

For very many people, work is a means to supporting themselves and they do not see it as having any other significance. And it may well stay like that, if it is useful, if it serves them. However, a lot who have embarked on a personal growth journey do think long and hard about choosing a form of work which satisfies them at a higher level, that has meaning for them, which they enjoy, that benefits humanity or the planet, that is somehow "worthwhile", that answers the call for purpose.

For some, there is a sense of vocation, as if they have been called to do something. It is as if there is some pull, or some driver, which attracts them to a certain kind of work. They "must" do it. There is an inner impulse. If you have this feeling, follow it. Something probably is calling you.

For others, it may be pure interest. This is usually a powerful source of enquiry. One slant on interest is the idea of doing what you love doing. Work that is enjoyable, that is uplifting, that gives pleasure, is frequently one of the most promising lines to go down.

In the real world

Activity: What work would you love to do?

....
....
....
....
....
....

According to Nick Williams[40], doing what you love is of central importance. In finding what we love doing, he explains that it can involve undoing our conditioning, our work-related attitudes, values and beliefs that do not serve us. We may need to adopt new values, for example. Also we need to find out where our heart lies and make that our work. This might mean having it that money is not the key issue for us, seeing instead that the world is abundant and when we follow our joy, abundance comes with it. As we have seen, working "on purpose" is central, but we will need to welcome transformation and change but also feel inspired to create anew. This covers much of what we have discussed on this course.

Of course, you could stay doing what you currently do. Maybe you need to look at your attitude to what you do right now. It could be that you have a lot of talent in your current work and you might benefit from bringing the principles we have discussed on this programme to that work. Changing careers is not essential, and changing how you view it might be all that is needed.

Money as an ego trap

In fulfilling our chosen direction, we often have to look at what we create that gets in the way, as we have seen with other areas covered in this book. This very frequently concerns money, or our perceived lack of it.

---

[40] Nick Williams, *The work we were born to do*, London, Element Books, 1999

Work, money and career

Money is arguably the single most important way in which we can allow the material world to de-rail us on our paths. It is enormously seductive.

"What good thing", asks the rich man of Christ, "must I do to get eternal life?" Christ replied, "If you want to be perfect, go, sell your possessions and give to the poor, and you will have treasure in heaven. Then come, follow me"[41]. The rich man was very sad, we are told, for he had great wealth. Another way of looking at this story is that Christ was inviting the rich man to change how he saw things and to shift his awareness from wealth to service, from the pursuit of wealth as a guiding principle in life, to that of the spirit.

We, in the West, have a society which revolves around values associated with money, wealth, success, economic growth, prosperity, affluence, the possession of material goods, physical comfort and all the trappings of what we've got or are seeking. We also in many places have a society that has huge amounts of unhappiness and suffering and is spiritually barren. It is also materially exhausting itself, as climate change is illustrating. These are the values of the orange meme according to Beck and Cowan.

It is founded on a belief system based on need and its concomitant, lack. Need is a core belief of the Ego. Walsch says[42] that everything that you currently experience in life is rooted in this idea, but need is non-existent in the higher scheme of things. As humans we do however think that there is not enough. Then we think we have to struggle for what there is. The result is poverty consciousness, either in us or as perceived by us in the world.

It is well worth thinking about the beliefs that you are attached to around money, because these will contain thinking that will ensure that fears associated with money will keep popping up and taking you where you don't want to go.

---

[41] The Holy Bible, Ibid, Matthew, Ch 19, v 16 and 21-22.
[42] Neale Donald Walsch, *Communion with God*, New York, Putnam, 2000

In the real world

Activity: Beliefs about money

> Write down all the beliefs you can think of that you can link with money or the lack of it. Include any fears that come to mind, particularly, because they often drive limited thinking about money
> ....
> ....
> ....
> ....
> ....
> ....
> ....
> ....
> ....

It is well worth getting a handle on what bottom-line negative beliefs you hold about money. Examples might be the fear of poverty, or of starving, as previous generations would have feared. In an agricultural society, which was the predominant form in the West until at least the late 19th century, starvation was a common occurrence. It still is in parts of the world today. Another money-related fear might be of failure, or of shame, for example in the fear of bankruptcy.

Often our thinking is closely tied in with our material aspirations. We can get so tied up in earning, day by day, that our thoughts can be absorbed in the material activities that go with it, making decisions about buying, making purchases, paying bills, scrutinising bank accounts, debts, and so on. This is survival stuff, pure ego.

Being aware with money

When we become aware, we can refocus our awareness on an approach which is creative, accepting, expansive, loving and enjoying. Then we can change our attitudes to money. Money is simply an instrument of exchange. Money flows in and it flows out. Our worth is not measured by how much we have. Our "net worth" is the constant filling up of love. Just that. The universe is abundant. Goodness constantly flows, as does love. It is generous, giving. We receive abundance and we give it away, in a natural cycle. To hold on to it stops the flow. We give thanks for what comes to us and we generously give it away. So, when you get paid, say "thank you" and when you pay your bills imagine yourself giving to the payee.

The key is in our thinking. Change how you think, and what happens will change. Think that you are successful, says Wayne Dyer in *The Power of Intention* and have the intention that you are attracting abundance. Think that you are abundant. And focus on your purpose and your joy. Let the flow of abundance do the rest.

Become aware, by witnessing, when your fears are present about money. Notice them, let them go, and refocus your mind on your intention to be abundant. Say, "I am abundant and abundance is in my life".

Activity: Being abundant

In what ways will you manifest "abundance" thinking in your life?
....
....
....
....
....
....

What intention will you adopt to support you?
....
....
....
....

Being on purpose in your work

It has already been suggested that you include your work and your career in your purpose statement. It is not essential. Some of you may not see it as important. You might not of course have a job or career. If this is true, you might be considering what else you may do, or may already be doing, that can have purpose. Can you think of a way of

In the real world

giving what activities you carry out in your day some meaning or purpose. There are those, for example who do charitable work or look after their family. They might give some sense of purpose to this.

People sometimes stop their work, as with redundancy or retirement, and then feel a strong loss of purpose. Others look after families but do not feel that what they do is "worthwhile". This is the time to really think about where meaning and purpose can be introduced, so that all of life has value. Your purpose then becomes a litmus test when choices come up about your work. Regularly you can ask yourself, "Am I on purpose here?" There are two particular ways in which people often see themselves in their work as being purposeful:

(1) **Personal power**

In adopting new choices about their work, many say they find they are being true to themselves at last; they are being authentic. They are doing something for themselves. They are expressing themselves as they truly are. In a sense they are stepping into their power. They are in control. They are deciding their direction and what they do. It is the principle of creativity in action.

(2) **Service**

Many choose directions that involve doing something that benefits others or the community in some way. They may perceive it, or even express it as being of service or being in service. This is not service, in the pre-20th century sense of the servant employed by some well-to-do person. This is service in the non-egoic sense of doing work that is unattached to ego, without expectation of reward, truly **selfless**. Swami Chidvilasananda, in *Seva creates a pond of nectar*[43] describes 5 essential tests for something that is true service or *Seva*:

  a. The attitude with which you offer your service
  b. The intention behind your service
  c. Your expectation of reward

---

[43] Swami Chidvilasananda, *Seva creates a pond of nectar*, in *Enthusiasm*, South Fallsburg, SYDA Foundation, 1997

d. Your willingness to offer service
e. The way you perform your service

The invitation is to look at your motives. Why do you do this work? If it is as a contribution, if it is selfless, if it is given without any negative attitude, if it is done wholeheartedly, if you are not driven by the reward, you are probably acting "in service".

Service is a form of practice of acting in awareness. It is a great way of noticing when your ego is at work! You don't have to be in the helping professions to be in service. It can be an approach in any work that you do.

When people find that their work is on purpose, meeting a higher desire, they find a joy in their work. It serves as another way in which they can experience who they really are. Work too is a practice.

Practice

Reference has been made to "practice" many times in this book. Practice is meant a bit differently. Here we mean carrying out activities in which you practice the skills of awareness described earlier. Various spiritual traditions speak of the activities of the disciple or the monk or nun as following a discipline, a spiritual practice. Those of us, who have chosen the "householder's" path, living by earning their own living, raising families and paying their mortgage or rent, can also follow a **discipline** or spiritual practice. This supports us in living in awareness in the "real world". It is a self-discipline.

Self-discipline

1. The importance of sustained practice

Practice is essential. These principles need to be constantly revisited to start to really make sense and to see the fruit of your labours. People may get an early inspiration and feel that they have at last found where they need to be going. However, the real test comes over time, when our enthusiasm starts to wane and the snares of the material world creep in. Remember the power of the ego. This is why discipline is essential, so that you can revisit your principles and check your life to see in what ways you are succeeding and in what ways you are still getting tripped up by your ego.

2. Discipline in practice

It is valuable to keep your focus on what you are trying to attain. There are plenty of practices that can support this focus.

So what practices do you intend to adopt that will help you stay on track. Here are a few to begin with, but you will probably add your own:
    i. **Meditation**: This has been described elsewhere in the book. Meditation is an invaluable way of becoming aware and

Practice

constantly renewing your awareness. You are training your mind to focus on awareness. The mind gets up to its tricks and you can witness that and bring your mind back to its focus, perhaps by watching your breathing or by using a mantra. Have a regular time each day when you meditate. Early morning or early evening is a good time, before the beginning or after the end of the working day.

ii. **Reading**: Support your practice by reading books that are in line with your path, that uplift you and stimulate reflection.

iii. **Keeping good company**: Regularly meeting with others who are like-minded and who can support you in your chosen direction. Look to your friends: are they supportive of what you are doing? If not, does meeting with them undermine what you are trying to do? If so, look around to see who would be more supportive and whom you could spend time with.

iv. **Witnessing in action**: Make a point of regularly noticing what you do or think or feel. The more you practice witnessing, the more automatic it will become and the quicker will you notice when your ego is at work.

v. **Keep a journal**: A great way of checking how you are getting on is to keep some kind of daily log.

vi. **Have a special place where you go:** Have a room or part of a room dedicated to your practice, where you meditate and where you can keep special or sacred objects and books. It could be your sanctuary. You might also go there when you want to be quiet, to contemplate or do journaling. The place will acquire a particular feel or energy in time.

vii. **Keep a focus on what is uplifting**: Monitor your thinking and feeling. Pay attention to what your mind is doing. Keep your focus on contentment and the other positive qualities we have described. So much of our society is focused on the negative. Deliberately shift your awareness to what uplifts you.

viii. **Have an activity where you can perform service**: Note the points made about service above. See where you can deliberately do things selflessly and have "practice in action".

ix. **Attend to what you hear, say, smell, see and eat**: Look at what enters your awareness through your senses. Does it serve you? Remember perception and the power of interpretation. Does what you eat do you good, and what you drink? Do the TV programmes you watch help you to feel good or do they stir up negative stuff? Do the places you go to support you in feeling good, or are they vexatious to the spirit?

x. **Care of your body**: Like your mind, your body too needs care. Many activities can support a healthy body and also support mental discipline. This is one reason why many have taken up activities like yoga or tai chi, which deliberately focuses the mind on body movement and draws us inside and into stillness. Feeling good in your body will support you in feeling good in your mind.

Activity: What will you do to support your practice?

....
....
....
....
....
....
....
....
....
....
....
....

3. Commitment

In all this, it is important to commit, to take action. Procrastination is a great enemy of practice: "Oh, I'll do it tomorrow". And so it gets put off, or is done irregularly and then hardly at all. The vital thing about practice is doing it regularly. This is well evidenced by meditation. Practitioners all stress the importance of daily meditations if you want to see real benefit. Once it slips, it is very easy to slip further into not doing it at all.

Activity: Commitment

How might you sabotage yourself? What do you know about the parts of you that are skilled in sabotaging your efforts? Write them down, so that you are aware of them.

....
....
....
....
....
....
....
....
....

Some people refer to the aspects of the warrior in the spiritual journey, one who dedicates him or herself to focusing on the task to defeat the ego and realise their goal, developing skill and utilising courage. The spiritual journey requires courage. Courage is often accompanied by doubt. It goes with the territory of the spiritual warrior. The warrior challenges doubt and does not let it get the better of him or her.

Life laundry

In being committed, we inevitably find ourselves addressing the real issues that get in our way. It is possible to find many on a self-development or spiritual path who are in denial, doing the worthy stuff but denying the rubbish that lurks in the sub-basements of their lives. Others see it, but they themselves don't, or won't. As a result, they live a life that at some level is inauthentic.

So, we need to do the laundry, sorting out the stuff and giving it a wash.

In the real world

Activity: Identifying the rubbish

Where in your life do you honestly need to do some work to sort things out?

....
....
....
....
....
....
....
....

If you are not sure, it can help to ask others, get feedback, attend a programme or get some expert help. The point about awareness is training yourself to notice how you show up; where in your life do you do things that do and do not serve you. At this point, you might have some blind spots. Check it out.

What can happen as you progress is that the real challenges emerge. They are not obvious at first, in the initial rosy glow of developing awareness. What really starts getting in the way after a while is probably the bottom-line stuff you really need to sort out. The key point here is to not resist it but instead embrace it: it's your way out.

So, what's on your action plan?

Activity: Some actions I plan to take as life laundry

....
....
....
....
....
....
....
....

The journey

In this book we have explored certain working concepts about personal growth. These have been tried and tested by many people. However, I would always say that this is not necessarily the only way, but simply one that many have found works for them. In the end it will always be your own choice.

This working model is:

- Awareness is the key
- The present holds potential for a new way of being
- Taking responsibility gives us power
- We choicefully create our experience
- We are not our Egos: we have a higher reality, where in some sense we are all One
- There is no one way: you choose.

What will you choose?

In this part, we have devoted a lot of space to the exploration of who we are. It lies at the core of this book. You do not have to belong to any faith or religion or doctrinal system. What we have looked at can be made sense of in your own way. As with all of this in life it is really your choice, since you create what you get.

Different traditions mean different things by the nature of the self. What we have explored here is essentially a non-dualist approach. We have looked at what is really an experience of a space that we each come to find in our own way and make our own meaning of for our own path in life.

Today is not the age of gurus, of inspiring leaders, of prophets. Although in the West people often speak of them, we now increasingly are being challenged to choose our own way. We can learn from them but now we make our own path. This is why so many people today are seekers, wishing to choose, to make their own minds up for themselves. We are now our own gurus and thus need to get in touch with our inner guru. We are today each finding our own truth. That is the challenge facing civilisation, to take responsibility and become aware - for our own Self's sake, and ultimately the rest of humanity and all sentient beings, since we are all One.

Facing and accepting its challenges

This path, of becoming aware of your Self, is not a cake walk, at least not probably for most people. Initially, on first contacting this material, you may feel very good, and that is great because it serves as an anchoring, a "re-membering", a re-connecting, for when you don't feel connected. Yet it is important not to be under any illusions about this journey. The power of the ego is so strong that, for most of us, we need steady practice and support from others of a similar mind. That is why in this Part we devote space to how we can apply the learnings and reach out to others.

I have stressed that the real test of our exploration lies when we meet the challenges of daily life. This is where we need effort and persistence. It is therefore important to be prepared for that.

Confronting your demons

When stuff comes up, it is important to face it and deal with it. What you are doing is facing illusion and discovering that it is just that, something we have created which is not who we really are.

You may well be tested. When we make a stand for something in life, the universe tests us. Then we have to stick to our truth. As Neale Donald Walsch says, as quoted earlier, "In the absence of that which you are not, that which you are, is not". So if you think you've become very inspired and enlightened, and yet have not really resolved your ego patterns, what you may very well experience in life is that which you are not. As Walsch says, it is a law of nature, to fill a vacuum. So often, people report meeting people who are on a path and yet have a lot of stuff going on in their lives. We need to treat them with compassion. They may be aware and be dealing with it as best they can. And they may be in denial of the darker side of themselves, their shadows.

Re-member and re-mind yourself

The word "remember" is shown with a hyphen because what is happening when we remember is that we are reaching a point of awareness, noticing what is happening and re-connecting with our Self. If nothing else, this very simple process is the most powerful and sustaining - remember who you are. Remember your purpose.

Keep your focus on that which uplifts you. For example

- ❖ **Have a spiritual practice that regularly re-minds you of who you are**
- ❖ **Give yourself regular time for sacred space and for going within**
- ❖ **Get to know that place within you that is pure love, joy, bliss, contentment, enthusiasm, and so much more**
- ❖ **Allow that place to grow so that it infuses more and more of your life**
- ❖ **Carry something with you that re-minds you**
- ❖ **Smile to others: give them your love**
- ❖ **Take that smile within you and give it to yourself**
- ❖ **Take time to be in nature and around other people and re-mind yourself of your connection with nature and with them**
- ❖ **Take part in activities with others that re-mind you**
- ❖ **Affirm, celebrate and honour who you are**

In the real world

Activity: Your conclusions and commitments

Make a note of what you'd like to commit to as a result of finishing reading this book:

Further reading

Any selection of reading must be personal. Here is a small selection of some authors whom I have found to be well worth reading and who have various takes on the nature of who we really are, both from Eastern and Western perspectives, and of how to attain and live as That. In truth, the range of written material is vast.

A Course in Miracles, New York, Viking Penguin, 1975
Akasha Lonsdale, *How to do Life*, Wiltshire, UK, EP Books, 2004
Daniel Goleman, *Emotional Intelligence*, UK edition: London, Bloomsbury, 1996
Eckhart Tolle, *The New Earth*, New York, Penguin, 2005
Jan Kersschot, *Coming Home*, Inspiration, Belgium, 2001 (Written in English, with an interesting bibliography). This has now been replaced by two volumes, *Nobody Home* and *This is it*, (Watkins, London).
Jack Kornfield, *A Path with Heart*, Rider, USA, 1994
John Rowan, *The Transpersonal*, 2nd edition, London, Routledge, 2005
Ken Wilber, *Integral Spirituality*, Boston, Mass., Integral Books, 2006
Marianne Williamson, *A Return to Love*, UK revised edition, London, Thorsons, 1996
Miranda Holden, *Boundless Love*, London, Rider, 2002
Neale Donald Walsch, The *Conversations with God* series but especially *Friendship with God*, Hodder & Stoughton, London (also in USA), 1999.
Nikki de Carteret, *Soul Power*, Alresford, Hampshire, UK, O Books, 2003
Ramana Maharshi, *The Spiritual Teaching of Ramana Maharshi*, USA and UK, Shambhala, 1988
Roger Walsh, *Essential Spirituality*, New York, Wiley, 1999.
Swami Durgananda, *The Heart of Meditation*, South Fallsburg, Syda Foundation, 2002
Swami Muktananda, *Play of Consciousness*, South Fallsburg, SYDA Foundation, 1971.
Tony Parsons, *The Open Secret*, Open Secret Publishing, UK, 1995
Wayne Dyer, *The Power of Intention*, Carlsbad, CA, Hay House, 2004

Other writers have already been mentioned in the body of the text. If you look in their bibliographies, that will open up other lines of enquiry.

Further information

To learn more about John Gloster-Smith's work go to

www.johnglostersmith.com

Or write to

The Empowering Partnership Ltd
21 Fynamore Gardens
Calne
Wiltshire
SN11 0UA

Or call +44 (0) 1249 813 188.